Chamberlin will always be, first and foremost, a willing disciple to the craft of storytelling: as a listener, as a fan, and as a practitioner. He reminds us that stories mend and stories bring hope. This book is a great sharing of a life truly lived with the everyday wonder and celebration of The Great Mystery. I applaud you, Ted, from one storyteller to another. This was a joy to read. Mahsi cho.

—**RICHARD VAN CAMP**, author of *Gather: Richard Van Camp on the Joy of Storytelling*

Storylines: How Words Shape Our World tells amazing stories about amazing stories. We tell stories all the time, for good or for ill, but *how* our telling places us in time and space, how listening to the stories makes us aware of our world or forget it in the telling of tales, is Chamberlin's mandate. And he acquits it better than any critic, historian, or politician writing today. You want to listen to him tell us his stories, all along aware that you are reading his take on why and how we spin our lives out in our world of words. The best book on narrative theory of the 21st century!

—**SANDER GILMAN**, co-author of *"I Know Who Caused COVID-19": Pandemics and Xenophobia*

I heard an Austrian storyteller describe storytelling as "the art of juggling with a knife and a balloon." With patient humour and an irresistible narrative voice, Chamberlin takes us to the heart of this dilemma. Deploying a lifetime's worth of stories as examples, his quest leads, not to answers, but to ever-more entertaining questions about the nature of truth, belief, wonder, imagination, science, and myth. He argues that the sharp edge of truth and the lightness of wonder come together in the mysterious traverse between storyteller's tongue and listeners' ears to create an ancient, urgent, and just possibly soul-saving dance of suspense and revelation.

—**DAN YASHINSKY**, author of *Suddenly They Heard Footsteps: Storytelling for the Twenty-First Century*

Storylines is an invitation to journey beyond familiarity, with stories' ambiguities as our guide. This book encourages me. It helps me embrace knowing and not knowing. J. Edward Chamberlin's words provide welcome countermeasures to fractious dichotomies threatening to overwhelm nuance and subtlety in our present age.

—**JOHN BORROWS**, Loveland Chair in Indigenous Law, University of Toronto Faculty of Law

Drawing on memoir, history, politics, literary criticism and personal reflection, J. Edward Chamberlin takes readers on a marvellous journey into the heart of stories and storytelling. The beauty of the book is its conversational style. Chamberlin has created a literary text that sings.

—**WENDY WICKWIRE**, author of *At the Bridge: James Teit and an Anthropology of Belonging*

Storylines is a most insightful and engaging book. It is a delightful combination of critical questions and courageous thinking. We learn from the many storytellers that have taught Ted including scientists, Indigenous peoples, and other authors. Ted ties each part of the book directly to a world lived large with fascinating leaders, issues, and struggles. For example, he observes that our storytelling about economic and political change has become both "a blessing and curse." In other words, storytelling is an act of agency to create the world and we are not only responsible for the joy that is possible, but also for the horrors that we inflict on others, the planet, and non-humans. This means that through thoughtful, brave stories, we can create change. Ted notes that "we don't have a GPS for the uncertainties of life" so we need stories to think through problems and experiences, and to imagine the future.

—**DR. VAL NAPOLEON**, acting dean and professor, Faculty of Law, University of Victoria

STORYLINES

J. EDWARD CHAMBERLIN

Story lines

How
Words Shape
Our World

Douglas &McIntyre

DOUGLAS AND MCINTYRE (2013) LTD.
P.O. Box 219, Madeira Park, BC, VON 2HO
www.douglas-mcintyre.com

EDITED by Jennifer Glossop
COVER DESIGN by Dwayne Dobson
TEXT DESIGN by Libris Simas Ferraz / Onça Publishing
PRINTED AND BOUND in Canada
PRINTED on paper made from 100% recycled fibres

Canadä

DOUGLAS & MCINTYRE acknowledges the support of the Canada Council for the Arts, the Government of Canada, and the Province of British Columbia through the BC Arts Council.

LIBRARY AND ARCHIVES CANADA CATALOGUING IN PUBLICATION
Title: Storylines : how words shape our world / J. Edward Chamberlin.
Names: Chamberlin, J. Edward, 1943- author.
Identifiers: Canadiana (print) 20230157424 | Canadiana (ebook) 20230158129 | ISBN 9781771623513 (softcover) | ISBN 9781771623520 (EPUB)
Subjects: LCSH: Storytelling. | LCSH: Narration (Rhetoric) | LCSH: Fiction.
Classification: LCC PN4193.15 C43 2023 | DDC 808.5/43—dc23

For Meg and Geoff and Sarah

and in memory of
Edith Cowdry Chamberlin (1899–1986)
and Edward Eugene Chamberlin (1903–1996)

Contents

CHAPTER ONE

Balance and Belief in Storytelling

MORTIMO PLANNO, ALSO KNOWN AS RAS KUMI, WAS A legendary Rastafarian elder who at one time was Bob Marley's spiritual advisor. I first met Kumi because of my interest in the traditions of story and song that Rastafari has sponsored, and over the years we became good friends. Like all Rastafarians, he was deeply interested in the Old Testament stories in the Bible, especially those stories of resistance and survival to which Rastafarians regularly turn in order to reimagine the captivity of the Israelites as the story of African enslavement. In those stories, they also find passages that prophesy the coming of a Black messiah, identified by Rastafarians as the Ethiopian emperor Haile Selassie, whose name before his coronation was Ras ("leader") Tafari. They believe those prophecies and psalms, those stories and songs. And they help them to live with—and to survive and even prevail over—a heritage of enslavement and exile from their home in Africa.

In a most unlikely collaboration, Ras Kumi asked me to help organize a gathering of Rastafarian elders in Jamaica

1

for a set of *reasonings*—theological interpretations, in Rasta parlance—of Old Testament texts. These reasonings are spiritual and historical explorations of truth and belief, and they are as disciplined as any scientific theory or scholarly interpretation or rabbinical debate, with challenges being both encouraged and respected.

Just as things were getting underway, Kumi pulled me aside and said, "Brother Ted, there's something you should know. There are people here who think the world is round. And people who think the world is flat."

Then, as I puzzled over what on earth he was telling me and why, he smiled and said, "Same people."

It was vintage Rasta wit and wisdom. And it was a storyteller's pure paradox, reminding us of the uncertainties that we live with. And live by. For we believe the world is round. But we also believe that we are standing right side up, not upside down as we might be if the world really *were* round. Which it is. And with that we go about our business, comfortable in a contradiction that sets both truth and belief on their heads—and leaves us with a good story.

Every day we comfortably embrace another storytelling contradiction, applauding the sun in the morning when it rises in the east and admiring it in the evening when it sets in the west even though we have known for over 500 years, since Copernicus, and for some people around our world much longer, that it does no such thing. We are the people Brother Kumi talked about, balancing truth and belief in stories we live by every day—and with whose contradictions we are comfortable.

That comfort involves another alliance of truth with what I will call grace. The grace that is wonder. And the balance that is wondering. Wonder and wondering. Together they are at the heart of humanity. And they must have been there from very early days in human history, for they have been central to our survival. The grace of balance.

We can see something of this grace of balance in the original idea of a round earth, which defied the many other accounts of our planet as a disc floating in water, or a circle or a square with a roof or umbrella overhead and water above and below, or a host of other early explanations that entertained the curious. One of the first Europeans to propose a round earth was Pythagoras, a Greek philosopher and mathematician who lived in the fifth century BCE, much longer ago than Copernicus. He did so because he thought a sphere was the most elegant shape, balanced and beautiful. But he must also have sensed that even if it was not necessarily "true," it would keep wondering alive even as it offered a new wonder. The ideas of science do this now, not by proposing one truth but by offering a balance between several truths, so that light is both a wave and a particle, and things can be in two places at once.

Comfort with wonder and with wondering is central to storytelling, sustaining contradictions even as it invites belief. What I want to show in this book is how such storytelling helps us by illuminating the wonders of our world, some of which we know only by scientific or religious hearsay, and by allowing us to wonder rather than worry. And right now, we need the comfort with contradiction that storytelling offers.

Storytelling doesn't eliminate the worries, of course. That would be inhuman. But it helps us balance these worries with words and images that offer sanctuary. Sometimes, as we learn when a sad song makes us feel happy or a scary story puts us to sleep, the sanctuary is in the contradiction. Such storytelling not only helps us but saves us, as it has done, not perfectly but persistently, from the time humanity came into being. Not the time when we emerged from the cave, but the moment we went *to* a cave and began telling stories in images on the walls and words around the fire.

★ ★ ★

The contradictions at the heart of storytelling that I am referring to—well beyond those about living on both a flat earth and a round earth—are often signalled, and their impossibility celebrated, at the beginning of storytelling sessions. "Once upon a time" was for many of us the first storytelling signal we heard, and we soon understood that it meant "right now." This signal introduced us in a kind of ceremonial way to the storytelling world.

On the island of Majorca in the Mediterranean, traditional storytellers begin a story by saying *"aixo era y no era"*—"it was, and it was not." Khoekhoe storytellers in the southern African Kalahari start with a single word— *garube*, which means "the happening that is not happening." And Toronto storyteller Dan Yashinsky describes how his Romanian grandmother used to begin her fairy tales by saying, "Once something happened. If it hadn't happened, how could I tell you about it?"

Part of the power, and much of the importance, of storytelling lies in the way it parades these contradictions and shows us (rather than telling us) how uncertainties give truth its storytelling privilege, and how this privilege is balanced by a deliciously uneasy belief that is encouraged, in another contradiction, by doubt, belief's fellow traveller. Managing this contradiction, and balancing truth and belief, is what storytelling does when it moves us beyond the challenge of "believe it or not" to the invitation to "believe it *and* not"—and we take comfort in a strangely nourishing defiance that seems to be uniquely human.

This defiance begins with language itself and with the contradictions that we confront when words and images (as well as rhythms and melodies and gestures and equations and many other forms of storytelling) both are and are not what they present—or, I should say, what they *re-present*.

This contradiction is hardly a trivial one, but it is one we learn to accept and to naturalize so that it becomes as much a part of our way of thinking and feeling as our five senses. We naturalize words, one of our first forms of storytelling, fairly quickly. But not always easily, for like the storytelling they generate, words are radically contradictory. C-A-T is a cat. And it is not a cat. Or to imitate those storytellers I just quoted, "it is and it is not" a cat. As a word, it signals a "happening that is not happening."

I had my first confrontation with this in grade one, when I got sent out of the classroom for my answer when I was asked what the letters C-A-T on the blackboard were.

"They are three letters on the blackboard," I said.

"C-A-T. That is a cat," said the teacher.

5

"It's three letters on the blackboard," I repeated with a six-year-old's dramatic flourish.

I won't go on. I was stubborn, and that day didn't end well. But by the next day I was fine with the cat on the blackboard. And the teacher seemed to recognize that I had overnight become one of Ras Kumi's people, believing in both a round earth and a flat earth and a word such as C-A-T that is both a cat and not a cat.

Much later, I was comforted by another teacher, Marshall McLuhan, of all contrary people. He taught at the University of Toronto, where I was a student, and one of his comments gave my self-serving grade one stubbornness a satisfying turn. "By the meaningless sign linked to the meaningless sound we have built the shape and meaning" of the world, he said, describing how we represent ideas and things in words, and how we make sense out of the nonsensical contradiction of language.

What makes such contradictions possible, as I have suggested, is *belief*. It underpins representation, and it enables storytelling. Whether it came before or after words and images, belief was—and still is—a fragile intellectual and emotional instrument of enormous power. Fragile because it is always accompanied by *doubt*. And powerful because we *want* to believe. After all, believing is at the heart of storytelling, and storytelling is at the heart of what we know, and what we need to know, of the material and spiritual world. Which means we *need* to believe.

And that, in turn, means taking risks. Hoping even when there is no hope in sight. Doing so might be indulging in fantasy, but it's a fantasy that we live with and live by.

For hope helps us survive. In the midst of the most unlikely circumstances, we look not simply for a solution but for a "reason to believe" in one (to borrow the words of the Tim Hardin song). And if we can't find a reason, we make one up. That's one of the most important—and one of the most dangerous—things that storytelling offers. Making believe. But there is that counterbalance. Belief keeps us going. Doubt keeps us alive.

★ ★ ★

It turns out that balancing and staying afloat are what life is all about. Therefore, it should be no surprise that this is also true of storytelling. "Give me a boat" begins a seventeenth century Scots lament. "Bound is the boatless man," say the people of the Faroe Islands. All islands share one thing: until very recently you could get to them only by boat. And since we are all islanders, more or less isolated from others by our separate selves, getting together with others has been a powerful inspiration for storytelling. As a result, the importance of boats has been with us for a very long time and acknowledges our need to be ferried across the gulf that separates us, one from another.

The first written word in what became the English language was recorded by a cleric named Gildas in a sixth century sermon. It was *cyulis,* the root of our modern word *keel*; but it referred then, and in some seafaring communities still does, to a particular kind of flat-bottomed boat. The Irish poet Seamus Heaney, who as an islander knew a great deal about both the troubles of life and the sea around his island, described a good life as one requiring a balance between buoyancy (which is how I think of belief) and a holding (like truth). A ship and an anchor. And if we are at sea, as most of us are, one way or another, at least some of the time, the only other thing we need (other than some manageable weather) is to know how to navigate.

When I began sailing on the west coast of Canada, the nautical charts of the Pacific Ocean that I used were filled with small islands marked P.D. and E.D. The first meant "position doubtful," and the second, "existence doubtful." This was the 1960s, I should emphasize, not the 1690s, and it was not encouraging. But it did keep us watching and wondering, for good navigation always involves both making believe and dancing with doubt. Good navigators would plot their course, just as a storyteller might, and they would do so in pencil in order to make changes as they became necessary in making up their navigational story on a chart. And at least in the old days before GPS, they used to say that the key to survival at sea was to admit that you were always almost lost, balancing the navigational storyline of the stars with the curves and confusions of the wind and the water. Navigators needed to believe their charted storyline and to balance it with a lifesaving dash of doubt. (Many of us still need this kind of balance when we navigate the internet.)

With a sturdy boat conveying words and images, with lifesaving stories and songs to anchor us, and with a good navigational storyline to guide us, we can get off the islands of our separate selves and keep company with others. This is one of the gifts of storytelling. It brings us company and often shows us how to keep company with ourselves. Some of the stories I tell in this book come from my family and friends and the traditions of story and song I grew up with, and some of them are from Indigenous and other communities around the world that I have been privileged to spend time with. But all of them, wherever and whenever they come from, keep me company. Oscar Wilde once said that the people he knew best were the ones he met in stories. He also said they were often the people he liked most.

The ability of storytelling to find us company and to connect us to the people and places in a story, or to the storyteller, probably began way back at the beginning of human time with a desire to tell others—in words or images or gestures or performances—about something we had heard or seen or otherwise experienced. Something wonderful. Sustained by this kind of covenant in wonder with the world, and with each other, humanity was off and running. And humans were just a little bit safer in a world they already knew wasn't there just for them.

It was and it still is no small thing when stories offer company—the company of people from all over the world, especially those who have gone through the same things we are going through. These storytellers say to us, "This happened to me" or "I know someone this happened to" or "This will pass, but not yet." Then, for a moment, or often much longer, we are not alone. Such company is often as helpful as a basketful of advice, and stories of old times and other cultures, as well as from our time and our people, can offer it. C.S. Lewis, who knew something about stories, once said that storytelling can "heal the wound, without undermining the privilege, of individuality. There are mass emotions which heal the wound; but they destroy the privilege. In them our separate selves are pooled." But in great stories, he continues, we become many individuals and yet remain ourselves. "I see with a myriad eyes, but it is still I who see. Here, as in worship, in love, in moral action, and in knowing, I transcend myself; and am never more myself than when I do."

★ ★ ★

Over tens of thousands of years, storytelling has taken a variety of forms and has served a number of different purposes, shaped by the different languages and cultures and circumstances of storytelling communities. But at the core, and in the beginning, there would have been wondering about the things of the earth and the ordering of the environment, as well as a fascination with the wonders of the sky above, the waters around and the fires that alternately startled and saved them. In addition, there would have been wondering about spiritual figures and forces that, through stories and songs, helped people manage the mysteries of life and death, mysteries that for all our scientific storytelling and spiritual teaching are with us still. People would have composed stories and songs that established the truths and encouraged the beliefs of their culture—beliefs about who they were and where they belonged on this earth, as well as in the greater scheme of things. And they would have come to understand that these truths were shaped by their people's languages and their imaginings, for they themselves were the makers of images and the users of words.

They would also have recognized that everything they knew about the world came from storytelling, and that there *was* nothing but stories and songs, and that it had always been so. The fighting and feuding of their ancestors relied on stories, and so did the hunting and gathering—for tracking was an early form of reading, of interpreting the signs of things that were both there and not there. And storytelling about differences between Them and Us was a survival strategy long before it became a competitive instinct. Such storytelling had the power to protect people from reality by bringing them closer to it. It became the music of what was happening. As a story took hold, people came to believe it was true, although there were probably some—the awkward outliers and determined truth-tellers—whose doubt would have brought balance to that belief. But they all realized that wondering accompanied wonder as surely as night followed day, and that by showing them how to believe and not believe at the same time storytelling also showed them how to maintain the balance between truth and belief on which their lives depended. And their happiness too, for they knew both joy and sorrow.

Thus, storytelling and human beings grew up together. Some say humanity began when our ancestors first walked upright on two legs. Others that it was our opposable thumbs, offering new ways of making tools, that represented a marker of the human species, although as we now realize it was not an exclusive marker. But whatever the sequence, the identification of things and events in words and images must have signalled an important moment in human consciousness and a new kind of connection with

11

the world out there. An impossible connection, it must have seemed, but one made possible by storytelling that offered them things that were both there and not there. Embracing this contradiction has been one of humanity's great balancing acts. Or maybe it was a leap of faith (*faith* being a word I will return to in another chapter). But whatever we decide on that score, it would have been nourished in the community of others, and it would have flourished in what I call the ceremonies of storytelling.

★ ★ ★

The connection between storytelling and survival is both communal and covenantal. But it is also competitive. Some forms of competition seem to be fundamentally human and, like storytelling, they often display either an element of play or a promotion of difference. But the competition I am talking about here is not a competition between Them and Us, but a competition between humanity and the world of wonders and worries that are beyond our control—the many such things that humans have always struggled to understand and to manage.

Some of these worldly phenomena are out there. But others—often the most dangerous—are within us. And storytelling, in paintings and carvings and the many other languages of communication, has often been humanity's first response. It has also been our best chance to resist the forces that threaten to overwhelm us—the forces that from a distance may seem like fly-buzzing inconveniences but that close up can leave us alone and afraid.

Dealing with these forces and the feelings that they foster is an intrinsic part of what it is to be human and an indispensable strategy for psychological as well as physical survival—the survival of a sense of self and of our species in a world that is at best indifferent and at worst combative. Stories and songs, both modest and majestic and in both print and performance, help us to counter these forces with storylines that free us from the bonds of everyday life. Even brief anecdotes are often a blessing. For the world has a way of insisting on itself, first compelling us to accept the terms of its inscrutable and imperious demands and then enchanting us with the delusion that these are permanent.

Submitting to that world and accepting its insistent authority takes us closer and closer to what Henry David Thoreau, retreating to Walden Pond, described as a life of quiet desperation, in which we are always under pressure to react to what is happening outside ourselves or inside our body or our mind, and where we are tempted to surrender to the first thing that offers us any prospect of survival or any sort of power.

It is through our imagination and a belief in the truth of stories and songs—their genuine truths, however momentary—that we can successfully resist the pressure of those seeming realities that haunt and harry us, and we can push back with a creative energy we have been given by storytelling. It is an energy that is lent to us at first and then becomes our own. It is not a defeat of reality—that is, the kind of relief that narcotics pretend to offer—but a bringing of reality into the kind of contradictory truth-telling of our

earliest experience of story and song, when beauty and fear,
and the satisfying and the scary, danced together in a circle
choreographed in our imaginations.

★ ★ ★

And it is this contradictory truth-telling that nourishes belief.
Did the Greeks Believe in Their Myths? asks the French clas-
sicist Paul Veyne in the title of a book he wrote. Yes and no,
he answers. It is an answer we are more familiar with than
we realize, for it is at the heart of many storytelling devices
such as riddles and metaphors, as well as scientific and religious affirmations where something is something else that
it could not be. Or could it? Yes and no. To take a familiar
riddle, has there ever been a chicken without any bones?
No and yes, though it's better known as an egg. Words do
matter. Are the Jesus of history and the Christ of faith the
same person? Yes and no, the Bible says. Is light a wave or
a particle? Both, say the scientists. Or on a more personal
level, is love really like a rose? It is and it is not.

But Veyne goes further with this and reinforces his
ambivalent answer of yes and no by noting that "legendary
worlds were accepted [by the Greeks] as true in the sense
they were not doubted, but they were not accepted the way
everyday reality is." The Greeks put the gods in heaven, but
they would have been astounded to see them in the sky. This
is a kind of truthfulness, a storytelling kind, that requires
us to use *our* imagination to make it real and to make it
true. All good storytelling has an element of wonder in it,
drawing a line for us between the natural and the human,

the civil and the uncivil, the secular and the sacred, the real and the imagined, and then showing us how to turn that line into a curve or a pattern. It gives us a way of saying "I believe" when we are not sure, of understanding every word when the words do not make sense. This inspired foolishness takes place in moments of grace and reminds us that such moments are always precarious and often downright dangerous. They build up even as they break down our sense of who we are and where we belong. And they keep us in a state of wonder, a ceremonial moment of release from the tyranny of reality into the freedom of the imagination. A condition that we have been familiar with since the first stories and songs we heard.

Oklahoma writer Joy Harjo, who is a member of the Muscogee (Creek) Nation, has a prose poem titled "Grace," which describes the dark times her Indigenous people have been through over the centuries. They were driven from their land in the southeastern United States during the 1830s and sent west over the Mississippi to Oklahoma, on what became known as the Trail of Tears. Harjo takes this up in a story about the struggle she and her friends just had during a tough winter in what she calls "the epic search for grace."

> Like Coyote, like Rabbit, we could not con-
> tain our terror and clowned our way through
> a season of false midnights. We had to swallow
> that town with laughter, so it would go down
> easy as honey. And one morning as the sun
> struggled to break ice, and our dreams had

found us with coffee and pancakes in a truck
stop along Highway 80, we found grace.
    I could say grace was a woman with
time on her hands, or a white buffalo
escaped from memory. But in that dingy
light it was a promise of balance. We once
again understood the talk of animals, and
spring was lean and hungry with the hope of
children and corn.

   A promise of balance. That is what storytelling is all
about.

Ceremony and Community

When Jonathan Safran Foer, compiler of the New American Haggadah *(the traditional guidebook for the stories, ceremonies and songs of the Jewish Seder), was asked by his son, "Is Moses a real person?" he replied, "I don't know . . . but we're related to him."*

W HEN I GREW UP ON THE WEST COAST, I WOULD GO TO sleep, after listening to a bedtime story that was both scary and soothing, to the sound of a foghorn as scary and as soothing as the story. The sound was both strange and familiar, and a weary silence eventually came over everything with unsettling seafaring stories slip-sliding through my memory like mercury. The poet William Wordsworth once said that he was fostered alike by beauty and by fear in the northern English countryside where he grew up, a place full of wonders and wonderings. The foghorn seems to have brought that kind of contradiction to me. It wasn't a thought or a feeling. It was a mystery.

So, at its heart, is storytelling. It is both a mystery we learn to manage and a promise of balance in a world of bewilderment, which may be why the wilderness fascinates us so. And for me there is still no wilderness quite like the sea. As the Newfoundland poet John Steffler writes, "The sea always quakes more than the earth ever has / and we live on its edge." With storytelling, we similarly live on the edge of reason when sad songs make us happy and scary stories send us to sleep. The consolations of contradictions. The foghorn as the haunting music of what's not happening—not yet.

The promise of balance is always a contradiction and a hope. "I was homesick," sang James Taylor—which was strange, he added, because at that time he didn't have any home. So he wrote "Carolina in My Mind" to take him there. And every time I hear that song, I go home along with him. Just as many Jamaicans do when they hear John Denver's "Take Me Home, Country Roads" sung for them with new lyrics by Toots and the Maytals. The storyteller E.L. Doctorow, when criticized for bringing characters together in his historical novel *Ragtime* who could not possibly have met in real life, replied, "They have now."

Now I want to take us to a much more familiar setting, described in a wonderful book titled *Suddenly They Heard Footsteps* by Dan Yashinsky. He tells the story of a typically Canadian storytelling ceremony at an evening campfire at a summer camp near Bolton, Ontario, where he was a counsellor. Another counsellor had just finished telling the tale of Old Man Bolton, a grim and ghostly figure who lived in the neighbourhood long ago—which is to say, before flashlights—and was said to do all sorts of frightening things, things likely to strike fear into the heart of anyone out there in the woods, especially now that the campfire was dying and dark had settled in. The counsellor finished the story, and after a pause designed to heighten the wonder and the dread of it all, said cheerfully, "Bedtime, kids. Off to your tents." Nobody moved. "Bedtime," he repeated. Still nobody moved.

Finally, a small voice spoke up. "Is Old Man Bolton still alive?"

After a pause, the counsellor said, "Probably not."

Whether or not it is acknowledged, "probably not" is at the centre of many stories. Also, of course, is "probably," and we are required to believe both in a storytelling dance. Believe it and not. Science offers one of my favourite dances, somehow creating the illusion that its stories are absolutely true when they are actually underwritten only by probabilities. Will my father's sturdy old desk, on which my computer and my books and a pile of papers now rest, suddenly disappear in a cloud of tiny atoms and sub-atomic particles and photons and mesons and other as yet undiscovered elements that modern science tells me give it shape and substance and character? "Probably not," say the scientists. And because they are good storytellers and make improbabilities disappear so efficiently and so elegantly, we often think of science as a story of certainties. It isn't. It's mostly a story of possibilities, both likely and unlikely, with new stories replacing unlikely old ones and new discoveries and inventions inspiring new storylines. And most of the time we believe them, although sometimes we decide to believe both the new *and* the old stories. A round earth and a flat earth.

The challenge for scientific storytellers is that their stories are often based on what might be called hearsay—evidence about something that happened, told by someone who was there to someone who wasn't but who is now confidently telling the "truth" about what happened. For scientists, their hearsay comes to them from technology. They have never been to the far reaches of space that they talk so eloquently about, nor have they nestled into the infinitesimally small spaces where the atoms in my desk dwell. But as with all storytelling ceremonies and their conventions we believe most of the hearsay of science, unconsciously echoing Dan Yashinsky's grandmother by saying to ourselves, "If such amazing things hadn't happened, how could scientists tell us about them."

For despite the widely accepted authority of scientific theory, and its commitment to the experimental testing of its truths, the uncertainties of "probably" and "probably not" and the contradictions of "it is so" and "it is not so" are unavoidable there. That is the nature of all storytelling. And this is even more apparent in legal storytelling ceremonies. No matter how credible a witness may be in court, a judge will often still challenge hearsay evidence, echoing the uncertainty of storytelling itself by saying "I believe you . . . But not your story." Storytellers in all fields and in all cultures have been dealing with this uncertainty for millennia. And their invitations—to a storytelling "happening that is not happening," for instance—alert us to the need to be ready to balance seeming contradictions, and to find a way to believe.

Indigenous groups in court are finding new ways of doing this, often turning to both old and new truth-telling methods. In a well-known legal case that I will talk more about later, the Gitxsan First Nation needed to establish exactly how long their people had lived in their territory along the Skeena river in British Columbia. First, they presented oral testimony that included traditional stories that chronicled the history of their homeland. They told one story about a presiding spirit of their land—a grizzly named Madiik—who was so offended by some of the spiritual and material insults to his domain by the people who lived there that he brought down a rockslide and flooded out their ancient heartland. This catastrophic event (like Noah's flood) heralded a new and more respectful era for the community and the beginning of its new righteous residence there, for which that storytelling provided a precise date— 3,500 years ago. But in court, the Gitxsan relied not only on the storytelling of their elders, curated with exquisite care over hundreds of generations, to date the rockslide but also on the science of geology. They drilled down in the centre of the lake created by the rockslide and brought up core samples to provide another dating, using the truth-telling methods of science. And 3,500 years ago was the conclusion of the geological engineers.

This compelling agreement prompted a crucial question: *Which* storytelling confirmed *which*? The storytelling of the elders, with its careful delineation of the generations

21

of families? Or the mathematics of geological science? Indigenous elders argued that each story was validated by the other, and that neither had a monopoly on understanding what happened. The storyline of geology was just as much the product of invention as the story told by their people; and the imagination of both storytellers discovered a reality. The same reality. Truth-telling, like all forms of storytelling, often involves such a balance. (In the next chapter we will see the storytelling of the prophet Isaiah in the Old Testament balanced by the science of geology, with rhyming truths that inspired a newly minted naturalist called Charles Darwin. Two truths? Of course.)

The Danish writer Jens Peter Jacobsen, whose work inspired artists as different as the painter Paul Klee, the poet Rainer Maria Rilke and the composer Arnold Schoenberg, once wrote a short story that he called "Two Worlds," but he said that if the language had allowed it, he would have called it "Two World." That's the contradictory world of storytelling, offering a promise of balance in the Two World we live in. The flat earth and the round earth. The world of reality and the world of the imagination. Reality insisting on itself, the imagination insisting on stories.

Negotiating a balance between the two is where storytelling begins for most of us, by helping us to make our way in the world as we learn to welcome surprise and to manage the unwelcome anxiety it sometimes causes. Our physical life and our mental health depend upon finding that balance.

★ ★ ★

Though we do not know whether images came before words, we do know that at least 40,000 years ago humans were drawing and carving images on the stone walls of caves and cliffs—and probably also on the sands in the desert and the shore by the sea, though these were, of course, soon blown or washed away. Nobody is quite sure why the people did so, and as with artists ever since, they may not have been sure themselves. However, the mysterious power of these images and of virtual representation itself (which we are experiencing again these days with our new technologies), as well as the secluded and seemingly sacred nature of the spaces where the cave images have been found, suggests that they meant something very important to those early peoples: a new relationship with the natural and supernatural world around them or within themselves, and a new relationship with each other in both ceremonial and domestic spaces.

They would have wanted to celebrate their invention by truth-telling, and perhaps even by boasting about their knowledge of the plants and animals they drew for these ancient images are often exquisitely accurate and catch a sense of mass and movement with delicacy that is rare even in modern photography. They may also have toasted the spiritual as well as material company that this discovery put them in.

Storytelling, pure and simple. Boasting and toasting. And truth-telling, for there is truth in all these images— the truth of their imagination as well as the truth of reality. Scientific truth, artistic truth, spiritual truth. And beauty too, represented in all these domains. Truth and beauty, in monuments to the human spirit and to belief. Documents of the human imagination, often in a time of grim realities. Storytelling began there.

The beginnings of words and verbal language are harder to trace than paintings and carvings and textiles for an obvious reason: there is no physical evidence. In the nineteenth and early twentieth century, there was a lot of speculation about the origin of languages. Much of it was fuelled by Charles Darwin's account of the origin of species as well as by the development of scientific studies of human habits and societies—and in some ways, just as importantly, by a revived interest in spirituality. One explanation that became particularly popular in Darwin's time, and which continues to have an appeal, proposed that language evolved from memorable moments when humans were startled by something: the unnerving sight of a strangely shaped cloud perhaps, or a shooting star, or the dread arrival of thunder and lightning, or the unsettling sound of a towering tree groaning in the wind, or the sudden flight of a bird. The importance of this experience was signalled by the uttering of a uniquely human sound that was identified as a particular spirit, a ceremonial "momentary god" of the occasion and its wonder. A representation of something both there and not there, introducing the contradiction that language and storytelling celebrate and offering a way of managing the anxiety of that moment by affirming the curiosity it awakened. Balancing wonder and wondering. Giving inhuman authority a human form in a sound, a gesture—a word.

Then came language itself, putting words and the gestures they generated together. This joining of word and gesture, some philosophers and linguists and anthropologists have argued, was there at the beginning of language. It is an idea that was given entertaining expression by the eighteenth-century scholar and scientist Giambattista Vico when he proposed that human beings danced before they walked, a suggestion that was taken up and expanded by many twentieth-century scholars of language. I like the way Vico's mind worked—he also suggested that the Creator in the world's various spiritual traditions should be considered a verb rather than a noun.

With language came communication. And such communication became a habit and a way of keeping company, celebrating what might be called a communion with others in the ceremonies of storytelling that shared experiences of wonder and surprise. This communion sponsored a sense of curiosity and a habit of wondering about things, and offered a crucial instrument for survival—a sharing of material knowledge and spiritual wisdom.

Taking this up, the art historian Ernst Gombrich writes (in a lovely book for young adults called *A Little History of the World*) about the importance in human history of what he calls "invention." Along with the making of fire for cooking and warmth, Gombrich suggests that one of the most important moments was when humans turned to gathering in small communities where they "invented *talking* . . . having real conversations with each other using words" and what Gombrich calls "names for things." In this way, words became this thing or that event, distancing humans from sometimes fearful reality by bringing it back to virtual, manageable representation—first in words and then in stories or songs, signalling the beginning of what we think of as human consciousness.

Eventually those wonderful first words for things, those momentary gods, slipped into conventional use and became what Ralph Waldo Emerson called "fossil poetry," mere relics with the imaginative life gone out of them. But story-tellers, probably from time immemorial, have taken pleasure in bringing that life back, making old words new again and refreshing language through the wonder of a "this is that" metaphor and the strangeness of a moment of encounter.

Sometimes there is a survival strategy involved in this kind of refreshment, as when Rastafarians turn words upside down to make new meanings, turning *oppression* into *downpression* (since if you are being pressed down the pressure cannot be up) and *understand* into *overstand* (since what we call understanding is just our way, which is to say our illusion, of standing over things). Other traditions take pleasure in refreshing the life and truth of language in other ways, and every age takes its turn with metaphor. So Robert Burns, writing for an eighteenth-century British audience, proposed that "my Luve is like a red, red rose," renewing their awareness of the beauty and the truth of love—and of roses. And while Burns's metaphor still holds our attention, the Spanish American poet William Carlos Williams, living in industrialized America in the twentieth century, needed something new. So he wrote "my luv is like a green-glass insulator on a blue sky," recovering something of the fresh-ness and outrageousness that we associate with being in love.

But since poets use words for a particular time and place and community, they don't always take account of the wider world. C.S. Lewis, whom I admire for many things, was not (and certainly never claimed to be) right every time. He once said that the great medieval poem "The Romance of the Rose" would not ring true if it had been written as "The Romance of the Onion." What he should have added was "not in Europe." For a romance of the rose might not ring true for other audiences when a romance of cinnamon and scallions might be just right, as the poets Michael Ondaatje (in "The Cinnamon Peeler") and Lorna Goodison (in "Guinea Woman") have reminded us. Refreshing language and its words is essential to good storytelling, while time and place are central to its ceremonies. And to belief.

★ ★ ★

It is company, or community, that usually offers encouragement for belief. But why is it that we are especially comfortable believing unbelievable things in company? And not just spiritual believing, in which a congregation often has a ceremonial place in storytelling. It is true in secular belief too, such as in the singing of a storytelling national anthem before a hockey game. That ceremonial suspension of disbelief (whether or not we pay any attention to the words) may have something to do with the comfort that company gives. But whatever the story is, and whoever we are with, saying yes to belief often seems to come more easily to us than saying no. We want to believe. We need to believe.

Things change over time, and so have the ways and means of storytelling and the character of its ceremonies.

27

But storytelling has kept its contradictory instincts and its enthusiasm for keeping company even as it turns to new subjects, new times and new places, new technologies and new truths that contradict the old ones. For whether in scientific explanations, spiritual ceremony or political challenge, in courtroom testimony or medical diagnosis or children's stories and educational texts, storytelling continues to be shaped by its role as the custodian of truth and belief. And it often returns to its roots by maintaining the tension its traditional custodians celebrate. It was and it was not. The happening that is not happening. Once upon a time is right now.

Telling stories, especially certain stories, in the company of others in a formal or ceremonial way probably began in the dawn of human time with gatherings in caves and on the seashore and along the riverbanks and by waterholes in the deserts of the world. These ceremonial storytellings eventually developed their own stern protocols. Stand up for the national anthem. Bow your head or kneel to pray. Put on your pajamas at bedtime. (When I was a youngster, if I didn't have mine on there would be no story.) Other storytelling conventions are as varied as the stories and songs they introduce, and often specific to the storyteller. The anthropologist Julie Cruikshank tells of listening to a Tagish storyteller in the Yukon whom she would occasionally interrupt to ask a question. Every time she did so, the woman would start again at the beginning.

I use the word *ceremony* to catch something of the spiritual dimension of storytelling, and I use *spiritual* in the sense that storytelling calls on *belief*. However, *belief*, in its everyday sense, has no necessary religious affiliations. And yet, to bring into play a word that we are sometimes uncomfortable using these days, storytelling requires *faith* in the ceremony that is being enacted. This faith is somewhat surprisingly true even in the storytelling of science, with many scientists echoing John Polanyi, the Canadian Nobel laureate in chemistry, who insisted that "it is not the laws of physics that make science possible but the unprovable proposition that there exists a grand design underlying the physical world. And not just any old 'grand design' but one that is accessible to the limited sense and modest reasoning powers of the species to which we belong. Scientists subscribe with such conviction to this article of faith that they are willing to commit a lifetime to the pursuit of scientific discovery." Albert Einstein added to this invocation of faith, insisting that "the most beautiful thing we can experience is the mysterious. It is the source of all true art and science."

Most of us also need this kind of faith not only to pursue scientific discoveries and better scientific stories but also to hope for better times for ourselves and for our loved ones and for our communities. Going to Carolina in our minds. Knowing (with U2) that we still haven't found what we're looking for, and that we must keep searching for it. Telling ourselves—with William Ernest Henley, the nineteenth-century author of the poem "Invictus," and with Nelson Mandela, for whom that poem was a lifeline during his twenty-seven years in prison—that we are the masters of our fate and the captains of our soul. We need faith as well as hope to seek out a better understanding of the wider world around us and of the mysterious inner world of our own thoughts and feelings.

The idea of a ceremonial element to storytelling, one in which contradictions become consolations, is often signalled by an introductory invitation into a domain where conventional sense and nonsense come together in company not only with the virtual or actual storyteller but also with that part of ourselves that loves the kind of contradictions that storytelling celebrates. The writer T.S. Eliot compared the ceremonial passage into storytelling with entering a *Sacred Wood*, which was his title for a book in which his signature essay, "Tradition and the Individual Talent," appeared. He was referring to literary talent in that essay, but with the musical hall as one of his favourite storytelling arenas, we can be sure he understood "literature" as an upscale term for the stories and songs we admire.

Growing up I was very fond of folk songs, which in many ways represent a definitive communal storytelling tradition. When I came to read literature, I often heard folk songs dismissed as not part of the family of genuine storytelling. But I had precedent on my side. When literature entered the schoolhouses and colleges and universities of Europe and the Americas in the middle of the nineteenth century, replacing a mixed bag of myth and history, philosophy and politics, singing and storytelling, it drew its early inspiration from traditional folk tales and folk songs. The first professor of what was called Literature (instead of Oratory and Rhetoric) at Harvard University in 1876 was Francis James Child, who became famous far beyond the academy as editor of *The English and Scottish Popular Ballads*, a collection of seventeenth- and eighteenth-century folk songs often referred to as the *Child Ballads*—the name itself an accidental reminder, if we needed one, that many of the oldest stories we know first came to us in the form of storytelling songs designed to consolidate a sense of community with their invariably universal storylines.

Together with his successor, the folklorist George Kittredge, Child founded the Modern Language Association (the MLA), which has become the temple for literary worship across the Americas and beyond. One of Kittredge's students was the celebrated folklorist John Lomax, who brought the storytelling of folk songs to the academy at the annual meeting of the MLA in 1909 when he spoke about and sang songs from his new book, *Cowboy Songs and Other Frontier Ballads.* Later in the 1930s, he brought the great blues singer Huddie Ledbetter, better known as Leadbelly, to sing his storytelling songs to that academic assembly.

One thing about folk songs all over the world is that they are not only communal but also ceremonial and, just like what we call literary storytelling, are all about lives and livelihoods, loves and losses, longings and lamentations. They come from community experiences with universal application, and they give them ceremonial form. Their seemingly casual tone often defies the circumstances they describe, confusing intensity and nonchalance—which is what T.S. Eliot once described as the signature of good poetry. And, of course, they were originally performed rather than printed, reminding us of the central place of oral performance in all communal and ceremonial traditions of storytelling.

The historian Donald Akenson notes that in his profession the founding fathers have generally been classical figures such as Herodotus and Thucydides, mirroring the dominance of classical languages and literatures in the humanities. "The classics," Akenson writes in his book *God's Peoples*, "were [to historians] so much classier as intellectual antecedents than were the texts that had their origin in the oral traditions of a group of Semitic nomads from the back of beyond." These were the traditions not only of wandering balladeers from medieval times and modern singer-songwriters like Jimmie Rodgers and Woody Guthrie and Pete Seeger and Bob Dylan but also of those who composed the Old Testament, the gossipers and gospelers of the peasant villages of Galilee. And that brings the biblical psalms into the company of rural folk songs and Delta blues and reggae, which may explain why the Bible has been so easily assimilated into many traditions. Such songs of the people have been around for millennia; the great Sumerian epic called *Gilgamesh* takes us back at least 5,000 years, and the stories and songs of Indigenous peoples take us much further back in time. One of the things I realized from thinking about storytelling in this way is how my involvement with Indigenous land claims flowed naturally from my interest in literature, for both literary studies and land claims are all about storytelling and community.

★ ★ ★

Whatever we call it, and however we experience that crossover into storytelling, the ceremony into which we enter signals *something*. That something is what children associate with stories at bedtime and what people from time immemorial have associated with communal singing and storytelling. It is what we enter every time we open a book or listen to someone tell a story or go to a rock concert or walk into a theatre or a lecture hall or a spiritual meeting-house to experience the truths and beauties as well as the brutalities and deceptions of reality given expression by the human imagination. And as Julie Cruikshank learned, it is important to not interrupt the ceremony unless its particular protocol encourages us to do so, as sometimes happens when a lawyer is presenting a storytelling argument, or a doctor a diagnosis, or a parent a plan for the day.

Sometimes it is the form of language—local or literary, professional jargon or scientific formula—that signals a different protocol. Scientific storytelling takes up a variety of specialized languages, including the languages of mathematics (as we will see—gently, gently, I promise!—in the next chapter). And such specialized languages require either an educated familiarity or a translation into a more familiar everyday language, which the best scientific storytellers do with remarkable skill; or else these languages need what might be called an audience's tolerance for ceremonial incomprehension. Many of the world's spiritual traditions use esoteric languages in their sacred ceremonies and prize the locations where these ceremonies are held. Changes can cause some pushback, as the Catholic church experienced some years ago when it moved from Latin to vernacular (local) languages in its liturgy, or when the location of the truth-telling ceremony in a major Indigenous sovereignty case had to be moved from the major law court in Vancouver to the small town of Smithers, where knowledgeable elders from the community could be present to "certify" the truth of historical evidence presented. And sometimes a ceremonial location can become fiercely contested, as in Jerusalem.

In other storytelling, there has been outrage when print has taken over from or overwhelmed performance. The Scots storyteller Stuart McHardy describes an eloquent complaint to the famous writer Walter Scott by the mother of the Scots poet James Hogg, a reaction to Scott's print publication of ballads he had learned from her. "There war never ane o' my sangs prentit til ye prentit them yoursel', an' ye hae spoilt them awthegither. They were made for singin an' no for readin; but ye hae broken the charm now, an' they'll never be sung mair." Scott had gone outside the original storytelling frame and silenced the spell, the truth-telling ceremony, of the ballads. He had broken the charm.

★ ★ ★

Some years ago, I attended the 650th anniversary of the founding in 1348 of Charles University in Prague. It is one of the oldest universities in Europe, and by the end of the fourteenth century, when it was just fifty years old, it had an enrolment of over 25,000 students, who came to the city to learn stories from the scholars who gathered there. But then things changed. By the sixteenth century, enrolment had dropped to under 5,000. The reason? Not boredom, that constant curse of education and its storytelling. *Books*. Printing had brought them into being, and "distance learning" had begun.

These days we are experiencing changes that seem as disruptive as those that occurred when printing came along over 2,000 years ago in China and 600 years ago in Europe. It's not the technology alone that is changing us and our storytelling. So are the ways, influenced and often invented by technology, in which we interact with each other. But this is not the first time in our fairly recent history that this has happened. The latter half of the nineteenth and the beginning of the twentieth century also witnessed a revolution in technology and storytelling, as Virginia Woolf signalled fairly dramatically when she wrote that "on or about December, 1910, human character changed," adding that "when human relations change there is at the same time a change in religion, conduct, politics, and literature." The date, seemingly arbitrary, was prompted by an art exhibition at the Grafton Gallery in London, which ran from November 8 to January 15. It introduced radical new forms of post-impressionist representation and encouraged abstraction in painting. Woolf would also have been very conscious of other technological innovations—photography, the telegraph, the telephone, moving pictures and other modes of virtual reality—that were altering the way people thought about what they heard and saw, and about what they felt about listening and reading, about "being there" and "not being there" and about "happenings that were not happening."

We still haven't caught up with the consequences of the electronic possibilities we have today, and "you had to be there" still finds its way into our conversations. But almost every day we are invited to expand our consciousness.

Storytelling will help us if we let it. And when storytelling comes into play, we will find ourselves—perhaps more than ever before—on common ground. That will be a comfort to many, but it will also be a challenge to some forms of storytelling and to Indigenous communities that are just recovering their identity. And certainly these diverse storytelling traditions will—and should—challenge any truth-telling that does not incorporate the dynamics and diversity of storytelling itself.

Computer technology offers possibilities with which we are just becoming comfortable and which are fostering new human relationships and new forms of storytelling— although they may not be as new as we might think, for mixed media have been with us for thousands of years. Changes like these can be disconcerting or exciting, often depending on our age and agility as well as our cultural conventions. Long before Virginia Woolf, Plato said that if we change the forms of imaginative expression——he singled out music—we change something fundamental in not only the artistic and cultural but also the moral and political nature of a society. Down deep, we all know this. It's why we sometimes react with such initial outrage to new musical styles like rock and roll or reggae or rap. It's why there was a riot at the premiere of Igor Stravinsky's ballet *The Rite of Spring* in Paris in 1913. Fortunately, that outrage doesn't inhibit, and often encourages, change.

But the sense of necessary civil and ceremonial discipline in storytelling ultimately transcends cultural differences and changes in technology. Something of its universal character is apparent in a commentary by the

Chinese philosopher Confucius 2,500 years ago, on how the correct words can shape or misshape our communities. It is the *idea* of correctness, rather than its different forms in different cultures at different times, that is crucial here.

> If names be incorrect, speech will not follow its natural sequence. If speech does not follow its natural sequence, nothing can be established. If nothing can be established, no rules of conduct or music will prevail. Where rules of conduct and music do not prevail, law and punishments will not be just. When law and punishment are not just, the people will not know where to place their hands and feet.

★ ★ ★

I am often asked by family and friends and politicians and taxi drivers what we do at the university where I taught for much of my working life. "We tell stories," I always say. Old stories—about the origin of species and the decline and fall of empires, about big bangs and small particles, about justice and freedom, supply and demand, economy and efficiency. And we make up new stories. We call the old ones "teaching." And the new ones "research." And we watch them compete for our attention, and our belief.

And as Confucius advised, we teach correct names and proper relationships in anatomy and astronomy, chemistry and physics, medicine and engineering, common and civil

37

law, praise and prayer, and we try to show how everything follows from that. This is why we emphasize the need for ceremonial discipline in the languages of regulatory regimes and religious faiths, too. For far beyond academic subjects, this attention to what we at the university call "disciplines" is what the protocols of all cultures are about.

What difference does all this attention to storytelling discipline make when the world seems to be tumbling down and we feel like we are falling apart? It holds us close to that world, and to each other; it allows us freedom to wonder within those disciplined storytelling ceremonies without being overwhelmed. This is the covenant in wonder with the world and with ourselves that storytelling offers. And even though a strong sense of ceremony doesn't always simplify our lives, day in and day out it saves them, and it saves us all from what the English poet Thom Gunn called, in a poem titled "On the Move," the "dull thunder of approximate words."

The regulation of correctness can, however, take its toll. Jacob (Jake) Thomas was a distinguished Cayuga faith keeper in the Iroquois Confederacy of six First Nations, the Haudenosaunee, and he was custodian of their Great Law of Peace. He had been schooled in its ceremonial storytelling formalities since he was a child. And he had learned them in his native language, deemed by the elders who were the guarantors of its sanctity to be the only language in which it was "true," the only language that could follow the natural sequence of the Great Law and ensure that people would know where to place their hands and feet. Once a year, Jake would recite it from memory over several days in the longhouse, the traditional ceremonial home of the people of the Haudenosaunee.

But there was a problem. There were only a few dozen native speakers of Cayuga still alive by the 1960s, and only a few more could understand it, so the Great Law was essentially unavailable to everyone else. Jake proposed to recite the Great Law in English, to make it known to the majority of those for whom it should be a guide—*the* guide—to a good and responsible life. But there was fierce opposition from the elders, so fierce that they banned him from the longhouse, his spiritual and cultural home. They underestimated his resolve. He went ahead anyway. And they pulled back. Then together they dedicated themselves to the revitalization of Cayuga among their people, especially the young people.

I knew Jake well, and a few years later I was asked by the Royal Commission on Aboriginal Peoples to gather a group of Indigenous elders and historians and settler scholars from across the country to discuss plans for an Indigenous history. Among the group were Jake Thomas and the distinguished Plains Cree elder and linguist Stan Cuthand, along with a lively mix of others from several generations and communities. We met for a week on Nakoda territory west of Calgary.

Just before we were about to begin, Jake came to me and asked if he could open our discussion with a prayer. Of course I agreed, and he began a prayer in Cayuga that was understood by nobody else there. But its request for help from the spirits in our deliberations and its message of respect to them was clear, and it established an unmistakable sense of spiritual as well as communal support for our gathering.

That evening after dinner, Stan took me aside and asked if *he* could say the prayer the next day. I was pleased and said, as I had to Jake, that we would be honoured. When the morning came, Stan began in a dialect of Cree that clearly confused the Cree speakers among us, but he displayed a similar spirit to Jake's, this time from a western Plains perspective. And it was a little longer than Jake's.

I sensed what was ahead of us. Over the next four days, we opened with Jake and then Stan and then Jake and then Stan, each prayer slightly longer than the previous one. Everyone understood. It was a perfect and, I am sure, a deliberate demonstration of something else I have mentioned that is central to storytelling. A competitive spirit. Not between spiritual authorities, of course—they were much too wise for that—but between storytellers. They were having fun, serious spiritual fun, but they were also turning our gathering into a constitutional and historical reasoning session—to use that Rastafarian word I admire—about First Nations sovereignty, leading us into a consensus that got everything about our discussions right. Most importantly, we agreed that any attempt to display the character of "Indigenous history" in the country must, first of all, recognize that there are Indigenous *histories*, each shaped by storytelling languages and protocols. All of them are spiritual, none of them the same as another, each of them pushing back against the imperial notion of a single truth about the past—or about the present and the future.

As a final gesture of genial mischief, when Stan was asked by a relatively young Cree member of the group, who knew his reputation as a linguist, which dialect he had been speaking, he answered—with the traditional solemnity of a mischief maker—"The dialect the Queen would speak . . . if she spoke Cree."

★ ★ ★

Later I will turn to the settlement of newcomers on Indigenous homelands over the centuries, and some of the storytelling that may help us balance home and homeland and reconcile the past, the present and the future of our communities and our country. But now I want to remember my friend Reg Greer. He lived on the farm next to mine, where his ancestors had settled in the 1830s. And he talked and told stories about horses like no one else I have known.

Like many great storytellers, Reg was strict about the place and the time and the circumstances for his storytelling, although he might have scoffed at the notion that his storytelling was ceremonial. But as with all families, there was a ceremonial discipline in Reg's farm family. Cats in the house, where they could sleep near the airtight heater; dogs in the summer kitchen, the catch-all room between the inside and outside back door for boots and bicycles and broken chairs and baseball equipment; and horses in the barn. Horses were his storytelling company, necessary and sufficient.

He only told his stories in the barn, and only at certain times of the day or in the evening. His barn had been raised by his ancestors, who came over from Ireland. It was built of old cedar logs, straight as a die and strong as steel and still smelling sweet a hundred years after they were set down on top of the fieldstone foundations, with siding of rough milled planks long gone grey but better than almost anything we have come up with since. Like all living things, these logs and planks breathed.

All his life, Reg had raised the cattle and pigs and grown the grain crops that supported his family, but horses were at the heart of the farm and of his life—and at the heart of the storytelling that took place in the barn. After feeding the horses—and he had many, from foals to three-year-olds and mares and a wonderful thoroughbred stallion named Tamarack, famous across the continent for siring big hunters and jumpers that won prizes at the top horse shows and international competitions—Reg would let them out into the paddock, watching how they went along and got along, for like people they had good days and bad days and occasional family feuds. After he had cleaned their stalls and done a dozen other chores, he would let them in again, to be let out to the fields later to exercise their survival instincts— with their big noses and big ears and enormous eyes, larger even than those of elephants and whales—and most of all to run and run and run, from time immemorial a horse's best defence against most predators. But it was in the barn that Reg talked about them, and about the past and the present and always about the future.

Down the alley where he kept his tack, and surrounded by a great audience in the stalls, Reg would sit and talk where they could hear him. Reg liked rituals, and he believed that the horses liked them too, for horses, like people, are herd animals. At almost any hour of the day it was early-evening dark in his barn, perpetual storytelling time, with the sweet-smelling winter hay bales cutting the cold that came up from the floor and down from the beams that held up the threshing floor and hay mow above.

To a background of snorts and nickers and snuffles and the lovely soft blowing sound that horses make when things are fine, he would talk about them. It was their ritual too. Reg didn't talk about horses the way he talked about other things, like baseball, which he loved; or his boys, with whom he had epic battles and lifelong friendships; or his neighbours, whom he had known all his life. And he didn't talk about horses as though they were people. Horses were horses. They spoke differently, they listened differently, they watched things differently, and they thought differently. That was why he sometimes needed a wee bit of whisky when he talked about them, which brought out some of the old Irish speech he had grown up with and helped him rightify things that had gone wrong. He liked to go over to look at a horse when he talked, even when he wasn't talking about that particular horse. It had something to do with a sense of solidarity in that secret society, that secret language of horses, and of horse people. But Reg was not a whisperer. Few true horse whisperers are.

As I think about the stories he told, I realize that Reg loved horses not only for the independence they gave him as a farmer, but because they bound him to his farm. To him they were household gods. Old-fashioned gods, long-memoried and short-tempered, mostly good but sometimes not.

And you could never leave them alone. Reg had not been off the farm for more than a day or two for twenty-five years. Horses needed watching. They needed talking to. And talking about. And he needed them.

★ ★ ★

Like Reg, sometimes I cannot stop talking about horses, so I'll add another story about horses of a quite different kind. A spiritual kind. It was early spring out on the steppes of central Asia, and a rider was herding horses down from the hills onto the open plains as the grass turned green and the sky took on a Buddhist blue. Standing in short stirrups and riding like the wind, he swept through the herd with a dancer's grace and a gymnast's daring, watching and listening like a doctor on rounds.

I had gone riding for three weeks in northeastern Mongolia, the heartland of horse cultures, with my son Geoff. Riding all day every day across two hundred miles of territory, we were guided by a young lad named Gohe. He was from one of the nomadic herding families who had moved from their winter shelter in the mountains to the open prairie a month or two before and were settling in for the summer season of calving and lambing and foaling and caring for the health of their herds. The Mongolian herder's life is hard and dangerous work, easy to exoticize but difficult to describe with adequate respect for the knowledge it requires and for the way in which it transcends material and spiritual categories. These Mongolian nomads are both dreamers and down to earth. They eat horsemeat and drink mare's milk, and they herd horses for food and as symbols of wealth and power. But like our ancestors who painted horses on the walls of caves 40,000 years ago, and like our children who put up wall calendars of wild horses in their bedrooms, they also celebrate the grace and beauty as well as the strength and stamina of horses.

One day as we were riding out on the steppes in a driving rain and fierce wind, several horses appeared on the ridge of a nearby hill with no riders or herders around, their mood restless with the coming change in weather and the constant sense of danger that horses carry with them. Gohe stopped, and for a moment he and his horse stood there as amazed as the cowboy gazing at the stars in the song "Home on the Range," or any of us singing "Amazing Grace."

"*Takh*," he said, pointing at them. *Takh* means spirit in Mongolian. It is also the word for a wild horse. Technically, those horses on the horizon weren't wild. Gohe knew that. And seeing horses on the horizon was certainly not unusual. His family had a couple of hundred horses in their herd, and we had already seen hundreds of horses out there on the steppes. But within that moment of wonder, I could sense not only his worry as he contemplated the threats to the semi-arid grassland steppes that he and his ancestors had called home and looked after in a remarkable tradition of stewardship for millennia, but his faith in the grace and beauty of horses—those horses, to be sure, but all horses—and the importance of a ceremonial moment. And to name it with that special word—*takh*. For him, for that spiritual moment, those horses were wild. The wonder of that moment, and the word he used to describe it, separated him from Geoff and me. It also held us together, as words and stories can do, in ceremonial company.

★ ★ ★

Storytelling has to satisfy the particular ceremonial requirements of its community. Correctness, as Confucius said, counts. During the winter that I spent working at the University of Colorado with the renowned Sioux historian Vine Deloria Jr., he told me about one storytelling occasion that failed to do that. It was an occasion he was not proud of. A cautionary tale.

He had been asked to conduct a series of television programs with elders across the United States about traditional tribal practices. Vine was widely respected, and to get off to a good start, he decided to begin the series with the Lakota Sioux, his own people, living on the banks of the upper Missouri River. Setting up the first interview Vine talked with several elders, and one of them—Vine called him Fred— agreed, even suggesting some ceremonies they might like to talk about. The camera crew arrived, spent the morning preparing, and then one lovely spring afternoon, high on the banks of the river with a view that Vine said was straight out of one of those nineteenth-century photographs taken to record the "vanishing Indian," Fred and Vine sat down to talk. Vine had brought some tobacco, of course, and they smoked it.

Then Vine opened the conversation. "Fred, I understand your people had some traditional ceremonies that took place right here, on the bluff. Can you tell me about them?"

"Can't remember any, offhand," said Fred.

"But . . . but . . . what about . . . ?" sputtered Vine.

"Can't remember," said Fred. "Nice view from here though. Hope those boys get some good pictures."

Vine tried every trick he knew—and Vine knew a lot of tricks—to get Fred to talk, including telling some stories himself. But nothing, nothing at all, from Fred.

By this time, the sun was starting to go down, and the camera crew, by now completely exasperated, started packing up. Just as they were almost finished, Fred turned and said, "Vine, did I ever tell you about the grove of birch trees down there by the river?"

"No," said Vine.

"Well," continued Fred, warming to the topic, "we used to take the birch to build our canoes from that grove," and he went on to describe how they would make a cut twenty feet long and strip the bark from around the trunks of the massive trees, a single strip enough for one canoe. And how they did it only at a special time of year, signalled by the arrival of certain birds and the location of particular stars, with specific songs and sacred ceremonies.

Meanwhile, the camera crew were falling over themselves trying to get set up again. When they were nearly ready, with light the lovely colour of early evening, they signalled to Vine that he should get Fred to stop talking and start over. So they began once more, with the sitting down, the sharing of tobacco, and the opening invitation from Vine.

"Fred, I understand your people had some traditional ceremonies that took place down there in the birch grove, by the river. Can you tell me about them?"

"I just did," said Fred. "Weren't you listening?"

Fred played them for three days, Vine told me, telling lots of tales about the Lakota traditions but not one on camera. They got nothing—or at least nothing that suited their purposes. The storytelling stopped when the filmmaking started. The same thing can happen when Indigenous storytelling forms such as totem poles, which were expected to rot away and return to the earth in the place where they were raised after their ceremonial time was up, are instead preserved in museums far from home. I can understand why that is done, for they are precious forms of storytelling that nobody wants to lose. But as Fred showed to Vine Deloria, we should preserve them in another ceremonial location only if their storytelling ceremonies are respected and those for whom they tell their stories approve.

CHAPTER THREE

Contradictions, Uncertainties and Balance

The modernist painter René Magritte brought images and words into contradiction with his painting of a tobacco pipe, titled "Ceci n'est pas une pipe." ("This is not a pipe.")

"That is not what I meant at all. That is not it, at all."

—"The Love Song of J. Alfred Prufrock," T.S. Eliot

RECENTLY, I HAD THE PRIVILEGE OF ACCOMPANYING MY daughter, Meg, on a visit with students she was teaching in Switzerland to the European Organization for Nuclear Research (known as CERN), one of the world's most important centres of inquiry into the fundamental nature of matter and energy in the universe. It is where the Large Hadron Collider is located, a twenty-seven-kilometre ring deep underground on the border of France and Switzerland that accelerates infinitesimally small particles of matter to a speed infinitesimally close to that of light, increasing this mysterious thing we call "energy." It then arranges that they collide with other particles to replicate what the current theory assumes happened when the universe as we know it was created in a Big Bang.

Explaining the project, one of the scientists who had been working there for forty years described how they hoped the results would confirm their theory, upon which modern physical science is based. Then he said, "Of course, we may be wrong," and broke into a wide smile, adding, "And wouldn't that be wonderful? We would have to start all over again."

That's the spirit of science and, at least in my rendering, of storytelling. Competition with reality and those momentary gods—here called energy, mass and the speed of light.

Like René Magritte, the scientists at CERN have painted a picture—they call it a theory, which means a view of things—representing something they believed to be there and to be true. It is a very good picture, a scientifically sophisticated story, of something. But what that something is they are not sure. Maybe they won't find out. And since all they have is stories, they will have to make up a new story, a better story. That's science. That's storytelling.

When we try to talk about mysterious subjects such as love as poets and Hallmark card crafters do, just as when we try to talk about life and death as philosophers and preachers do, or infinitesimally small particles and infinitely large galaxies as scientists do, we often end up sounding like J. Alfred Prufrock: "That is not what I meant at all. That is not it, at all." But scientists are very good storytellers, and at their best, they invite us to join them in a moment of wonder at the mysteries of the world often long before they have an explanation, or even a name, for those mysteries, opening our thoughts and feelings to uncertainties and contradictions at the heart of things. It is as though we are on the shore with those scientists between the land where we feel at home, even when we are lost, and the wide water that fascinates even as it often fools us. That's where storytelling comes in. It is our landline and our lifeboat.

For storytelling ennobles wonder, wonder stimulates wondering, and together they inspire curiosity, which can be both lifesaving and life-threatening, but is one of the signatures of humanity. And it offers that promise of balance that Joy Harjo spoke about, the balance between wonder and wondering, between human life and the life around us on the land and the seas and in the air.

When the prestigious *Edinburgh Encyclopaedia* (at the time the chief competition to the *Encyclopedia Britannica*) wrote about scientific matters in the early nineteenth century, it was under the umbrella of "Curiosities," collected together as what it called "Rational Recreations . . . founded on some scientific principle or tending to illustrate some scientific doctrine." The words were well chosen, even if accidentally so, for good stories in science like those in all the other domains of storytelling are reasonable and sometimes marvellously unreasonable *re-creations* of reality, animating inquiry and inspiring invention that often changes our sense of the real and the imagined. And as the word *recreation* suggests, such stories also give us pleasure which, as much as new knowledge, is always welcome and often desperately needed.

Some would say that science looks after our rational recreations and pleasures while religion and the arts attend to our irrational ones. But as we know, and as that CERN scientist demonstrates, science has more than its share of irrationality, sustained by what I described in the previous chapter as faith. And science also has a good supply of lovely surprises, giving us the satisfaction of wonder as well as the kind of wondering in which thought and feeling come together. Which is where they belong. Together again. After all, they were together at the beginning of the experience of human life, and they are together in early experiences of storytelling for each of us.

If we separate thought and feeling we get the kind of amazement that is satisfied with the first explanation, or the kind of curiosity that is incapable of genuine surprise and therefore of serious inquiry. And we risk ignoring the uncertainties and contradictions that are part of being human, and that often leave us at a loss for words. Here storytelling comes into its own and comes to our rescue— celebrating uncertainty and cultivating contradiction and offering balance.

Wonder and mystery, of course, come in various guises and do not always fall neatly into scientific or religious or artistic arrangements. Although its languages take some learning, science's storytelling is not intrinsically more difficult to explain than the stories of religion and the arts, which is why interpretation has become a major industry in all of these arenas. What they have in common, to repeat my mantra, is an invitation to wonder and to wondering. Sooner or later "every valley shall be exalted, and every mountain and hill shall be made low; the crooked shall be made straight," said the prophet Isaiah. Sounds absolutely bonkers. But the geologist Charles Lyell said the same thing in his newly minted scientific words when he wrote his landmark book on the *Principles of Geology* in the 1830s.

Charles Darwin took Lyell's book with him on his great voyage of discovery that included his visit to the Galapagos, and both that book and, in a contrary way, the Bible inspired his thinking about the origin of species. And then he turned to the arts. On his return from that voyage, he referred to what he called the "pleasure of the imagination" that his experiences gave him, admitting that even after all his geological speculations (he began that journey as a geologist and ended up as a naturalist), he still had an "ill-defined notion of land covered with ocean, former animals, slow force cracking surface." Putting both religion and science to the side for the moment, he concluded that it was all "truly poetical." His wonder, as well as his wondering, would soon be writ large in *On the Origin of Species*—a poetic as well as a scientific story.

★ ★ ★

The storytelling ceremonies of science and religion and the arts—each with its own procedures and protocols—give us a way of retaining a sense of uncertainty and, like sailors navigating in foggy weather, a way of not being overwhelmed by the difference between being sure and not sure even when we are conscious of the consequences. These ceremonies build up our sense of who we are and where we belong and help us make choices.

They cannot make these choices for us, but they can and do help us understand what is at stake. How sometimes lost is better—and usually more interesting—than found. How every choice is in some measure caught up in a relationship between the ways in which we see the world and the ways in which we say things about it. And how curiosity both rules and rewards us in storytelling.

Like curiosity, uncertainty is an old, old story in human history, and it has been inscribed as the way of the world for millennia. Lewis Hyde, in his thoughtful book *Trickster Makes This World: Mischief, Myth, and Art,* writes about how Greek philosophy had uncertainty and disorder as fellow travellers with certainty and order, just as doubt is a fellow traveller with belief. He also writes about how myths around the world have frequently contradicted any attempt to impose certainty. As examples he gives the goddess of motherhood in Norse mythology, Frigg, who cannot save her adopted son Loki from danger; and the trickster Raven, celebrated by the Indigenous people of the north Pacific coast, who introduces deception and disorder into a world that he himself created and to which he brought life-giving light. If an orderly life could be ensured, Hyde writes, "the world as we know it would no longer exist."

Let's pretend we find ourselves at sea in a book or a boat, taken up and taken over by its storytelling (for boats tell stories too). Wherever we are, we aren't sure where that is, and sooner or later we need to navigate back to land and its modest but familiar certainties. We trust the storyteller to get us there. But storytellers, like boats, sometimes leave us to find our way on an open sea of uncertainties.

In Chapter One, I mentioned my early amateur seafaring and the navigation charts that were filled with the markings "position doubtful" and "existence doubtful," storytelling guides to possible rocks or reefs. That kind of uncertainty continued until GPS, with weather now taking up much of the uncertainty when it comes to sailing on the seas (and these days it does a good job of that on land as well). But we don't have a GPS for the uncertainties of life, and I doubt—and to be honest, I hope—we never will have one. In any event, old-fashioned navigation at sea may be more central to our contemporary consciousness than we realize, for its origins go back to finding the way across the desert or the tundra or the steppes or over the mountains or through the forest or the jungle. And then finding our way back home, even when home itself can be as contradictory and uncertain a place as we can imagine.

I will be taking up the story of Indigenous homelands in the next chapter, but the idea of home can be a very complicated one for some of us in settler society—either warm and suggestive or cold and distant. It is where we hang our hat, or where our heart is, or the place we must leave behind and lose in order to find ourselves. It may be right here or over there; here below or up above; real or imagined; in our past or in our future; a place we dream of or one we dread. It may be where we choose to live, or where we are chosen to live by birth or the blessings of our Creator.

Home may be all of these places, or none of them. In many ways, it is the incarnation of our contradictory story-telling imagination, both defying and transcending the reality of our circumstances. And it is caught with perfectly contradictory grace in the opening words of "Home on the Range," played as the last song at country dances in the west when I was growing up (and probably written, folk song historians tell me, in the 1870s by a saddlebag physician riding the western plains). "Oh, give me a home where the buffalo roam." That rhyme—*home* and *roam*—catches the contradiction: bound together by their sound, their senses pull in opposite directions. Settling down and wandering. It's hard to imagine a more fundamental contradiction, and we underestimate those who first sang that song almost a 150 years ago and those who still sing it today if we don't accept that our imaginations take in this contradiction every time the rhyme is recited. And then we imagine the amazing grace of the stars we gaze at in the night sky, feeling the presence of a permanent spirit in that moment of won-der—a momentary god——and knowing as surely as we know anything that its glory exceeds ours. We don't remem-ber those lines because they tell one truth about ourselves but because they tell contradictory truths about our human condition and offer another kind of balance between the sovereignty of our self and its surrender to the beauty and truth of the world. If we try to eliminate this kind of contra-diction, we are trying to straighten out a curve that defines us as human.

★ ★ ★

Whether we are at home or away "roaming," we use navigation every day. For me, it is always comforting to remember that ocean navigators plot their position on navigational charts in pencil to facilitate changing their course. For just as there is never certainty navigating at sea, neither is there on land or in life. We know this from the surprising and sometimes startling uncertainties that life offers. And realizing this helps us make our way to safe harbour somewhere, if only in our mind.

Different seafaring cultures, like different storytelling traditions, offer different methods of navigation and different sorts of "plots." The one I grew up with had its own tricks of the trade. Out of sight of land and anywhere the fog comes rolling in, you used to have to know dead reckoning. It's not a cheerful phrase. Some say it's just a misspelling of the abbreviation *ded* for reckoning by deduction. But whatever its etymology, dead reckoning was for centuries a standard method of calculating one's position by estimating speed and direction over time while correcting for winds and tides and currents. It was essentially unchanged since well before Columbus used it to navigate the Atlantic Ocean and the Caribbean Sea.

There are, of course, differences in navigational concepts around the world, but the most radically different were perhaps those used to navigate the great oceans of the world—by Polynesian sailors for millennia, and by European sailors since the fourteenth and fifteenth centuries. Both were remarkable, and both relied on observations of the passage of the sun and the movement of the moon, the planets and the stars, as well as the water currents and colours, wave configurations and prevailing winds. But the differences in technologies of observation and seafaring craft aside, there was one fundamental difference between European and Polynesian navigation. For the Polynesian navigator, the boat was imagined as *fixed* while everything else was in motion, with the sun and the moon and stars as guides and a matrix of ocean islands rather than some stationary mainland providing *moving* points of reference, like a plotline. For the European navigator, on the other hand, the *boat* was moving, with everything else fixed at any given moment on a map or in relation to the sun or stars in the sky.

In some ways the difference between the two navigational methods is also comparable to that between stories where the narrator is within the storyline and those where the narrator is outside of it—or between a spinning round earth and a stationary flat one. And this conjures up a very old question about storytelling, as baffling as ocean navigation. Is the heart of a story the storyteller, the story itself or the storytelling? The teller or the tale or what the tale is about? And with this, there is a question that has troubled readers and listeners for ages, probably since the beginning of storytelling: where in this triad is what we might call the "spirit" of a story or a song, the essential centre of its appeal? It is another uncertainty we live with. And thrive on.

One thing is clear. As technologies change, so do stories, and with them the balance between the teller and the tale and its topic. With the arrival of some current technologies that seem to diminish uncertainties, many contemporary storytellers compensate by intensifying uncertainty in their storylines. To the delight of their readers and listeners, I might add, who may instinctively recognize that we *need* experience with uncertainty to survive, and that stories and songs must provide that for us. As they always have, more or less.

But back to old-fashioned navigation and the managing of uncertainties. My friend the author and teacher and maritime navigator Robert Finley probably knows as much about these as anybody, some of his knowledge finding its way into his marvellous book titled *The Accidental Indies* about Columbus and the uncertainties and contradictions of his infamous voyage. Finley writes how he learned from his father about dead reckoning, with its "arcane formulas for triangulation and drift, for calculating speed through the water and speed over the ground, its tables, its protocols for record keeping, and its wonderful instruments of divination: the compass, the dividers, the parallel rules, the chart with its compass rose and its mysterious symbols, the taffrail log, the chronometer." It is a ceremony that sounds almost spiritual, using instruments of divination to guide us "out of the swing of the sea," as Gerard Manley Hopkins imagines in his poem "Heaven Haven." And indeed, like all storytelling, secular or sacred, it does depend upon faith and hope and a set of ingenious figurations.

But the results of dead reckoning manage the uncertainties even as they intensify them, for as Finley goes on to explain, the conclusions come to the navigator

> more in the form of a rhetorical than a mathematical position. In dead reckoning, as long

as you can see and identify landmarks, you
can fix a position, but as soon as you are out of
sight of land, or the fog comes in, your sense
of where you are depends on a single thread of
narrative you spin as you go along . . . Good
navigation relies on having good arguments
for where you think you are, but a willingness
to change your mind quickly . . . when things
take a sudden and surprising turn [and] you
are severed from a world you had understood
to be out there . . . All of the usual reference
points become uncertain . . . You imagined a
bell-buoy, the opening of a known harbour, a
white house on a hill . . . Instead, [there is]
a line of surf, a broken wall of cliff looming
above you, or worst of all, sudden green water
[signalling an iceberg].

This is storytelling at its most compelling. "There is
something interesting that happens in the moment of sudden realization that things are not as you had thought them
to be," Finley adds.

In a way it is as though you had been posed
a difficult riddle, a "who am I" riddle, where
you yourself are the subject, and you find
yourself entirely caught up in arriving at its
solution. This moment can be at once terrifying and strangely liberating. Before a solution
is found, this "riddle", for a giddy moment,

opens the world to outlandish possibilities:
since you are not where you thought you were,
you might, for a moment, be anywhere at all.

This moment of wonder, this lost-and-not-yet-found
moment, is a moment that storytelling has always fostered,
and one that is not incidental to the obscurity we find in certain stories and songs. Some of this obscurity is an excuse
for shoddy craft, of course——as, sometimes, is getting lost
at sea or crashing into the cliff. But much of it is inseparable
from the mysteries of language or the menaces of seafaring.
We go to sea deliberately, but we also plan to return. And in
order to do so safely, we must believe in the language of our
navigation with all its storytelling fundamentals.

That feeling of being lost, or almost lost, is very much
part of our experience, and we become familiar with it from
the stories we hear when we are very young. It's not all bad,
that feeling. It sometimes offers a kind of contradictory
consolation, a comfort of being at sea in a story, which has
been humanity's best way of managing being lost since well
before modern times.

The word *disoriented*, for example, which we often use
to describe how we feel when we're not sure where we are,
was first coined centuries ago to describe the experience
of venturing far from a centre of certainties. For medieval
Christian, Jewish and Islamic sailors who went out from the
Mediterranean onto the Atlantic Ocean, that centre was in
the east, the Orient as it had come to be called, which they
identified as their spiritual as well as their secular home.
If they ventured too far into the western sea, which the

daring—or, we might say, the courageous and the crazy—among them often did, it was said that they would become "dis-oriented," lost, and faced with the challenge of finding their way home. The far reaches of the Atlantic—not so far by our standards but beyond the end of the earth in medieval times—were called the Green Sea of Gloom by Islamic scholars and sailors of the time. To go into this watery domain was thought to be evidence of insanity, and if by some strange chance you returned, your civil rights could be suspended.

Portuguese sailors, who tested their limits sailing south into the then unknown, came up with a similar word to describe how they felt when they were far from their northern home and the North Star by which they navigated. They said they were *desnorteados*. Dis-northered. Like *disoriented*, *desnorteados* still has currency as a synonym for being, well, at sea in a story where nothing is sure because everything is moving—the boat, the wind, the waves, the current, the tide, the stars—and where surprises are always waiting for you in the fog. Something like life.

Being disoriented has negative connotations for us personally, but on the positive side, it is nothing more or less than being uncertain about things and being surprised by new things. It also reminds us of the importance of a sense of a centre, a North Star, a source of spiritual or imaginative assurance, a home, however we conceive it.

The German language helps us here, for it has two words for disorientation, or alienation as we sometimes call it: *verfremdung*, the good kind, and *entfremdung*, the bad. The good kind is what I am talking about, what literary scholars refer to as "defamiliarization," "making strange," or what the twentieth-century playwright Bertolt Brecht called "distancing." We need to give such distancing its due since it makes it possible for us to sing a sad song and feel happy, or to hear a scary story with pleasure, or to enjoy a frightening surprise. And distancing is also what we achieve when we watch a play or a movie and spectator decorum inhibits us from running onto the stage to warn the heroine or interrupt the storyteller. We learn all this as children, not always perfectly, but usually in time for the second act in life.

Occasionally, as in the late nineteenth and early twentieth century, uncertainty rules rather than reinforces storytelling. Stories and songs and paintings and carvings and music and dance joined hands with new forms of spiritual inquiry and sometimes with the sciences to celebrate uncertainties. E.M. Forster did this with the Marabar Caves, in his novel *A Passage to India*, and many other novelists from Marcel Proust to James Joyce explored it in their storytelling. Painting did the same thing in the early twentieth century with abstraction (which had been around for millennia and will always have a place in visual storytelling, but still seems to have startled many people). Musicians did it with a variety of new tonal and instrumental experiments; Helena Blavatsky and Rudolf Steiner did it with theosophy and anthroposophy; and the physicist Werner Heisenberg did it with what became known as the uncertainty principle, asserting that it is impossible to know both the position and the movement of the elements such as electrons and atoms that make up reality because they are, according to modern science, *both* particles and waves.

These confusions were intensified by new technologies, including those of new mathematical languages, that gave virtual presence to actual sights and sounds, making it at least imaginatively possible to be in two places at once. We are still living through this revolution. The uncertainties of form and function in contemporary storytelling may be helping us balance the perennial "probablys" and "probably nots" of life by keeping us company. Which is where storytelling began.

★ ★ ★

Now to riddles, which Robert Finley mentioned a moment ago to describe the experience of being disoriented. Riddles are one of our oldest forms of story and song, perhaps as old as language itself when those momentary gods, the first words, challenged us to believe that a word or image was something else it clearly was not—a bolt of lightning or a peal of thunder or a beautiful birdsong or whatever it was that caused that moment of wonder. And a single word inspired us to believe it and not.

One group of early and still very common riddles give a nod to this possible origin of language by setting words and images into a kind of competition. In his book *Roots of Lyric*, Andrew Welsh gives a set of examples of riddles of this kind, one of which, an Irish riddle for snow, gives a picture and then a paradox:

> A milkwhite gull through the air flies down,
> And never a tree but he lights thereon.

And William Wordsworth's famous "crowd, / A host, of golden daffodils; / Beside the lake, beneath the trees, / Fluttering and dancing in the breeze" recalls a long tradition of riddling, represented by this description of a field of flax from Maryland folklore.

> Out in the garden
> I have a green spot,
> And twenty-four ladies dancing on that;
> Some in green gowns,
> And some in blue caps.
> You are a good scholar
> If you riddle me that.

These each follow a familiar pattern for riddles, in which wonder is offered not only as a charming moment but as a challenge, with the stakes higher than they might seem. Even everyday riddles such as these from Francis James Child's Ballad #46, which have long since found a place in popular folklore, follow this pattern:

> I must have to my supper
> A chicken without a bone,
> And I must have to my supper,
> A cherry without stone.

Such riddles present a competitive conflict at the soul of storytelling. If we cannot figure out such riddles, we get to wondering what we really know about what we call reality, and whether the meanings that we take for granted in the words and images we use to describe and decipher reality are meaningless after all. Riddles present us with a radical choice. On the one side, we can take a riddle as given and change our common sense understanding of the world, an understanding that may have served us pretty well up to now and change would be disconcerting, if not disastrous. Or on the other side, we could solve the riddle, chuckling with pleasure at our cleverness and expanding our interpretation of words. Until we make this choice, we find ourselves lost, in a nonsense moment stranded between kinds of knowing. A mysterious moment both worrying and wonderful. A moment of both panic and a kind of peace, free from the relentless authority of both words and the world. A lovely moment, sometimes. A very lonely one, at other times.

In this way, riddles test the authority of words and the world, which is to say, of the imagination and reality. Can that challenge be used to change reality? Yes and no. And in between those alternatives, the challenge can cause us some worrisome moments of wonder. In the case of most riddles, it is the words that lose the struggle and reality that wins— as when we come up with "an egg" and "cherry blossoms" as answers for the riddles I just mentioned.

But not always. The riddles of religion and science are sometimes more likely to encourage us to jettison the words and go with a new conception of the world, and the riddle of infinity has never been settled and has never left the stage, as we will see in a moment. But all riddles highlight the precarious nature of our knowledge of the world and its dependence on words and images and on the stories they tell. And riddles remind us how crucial it is to balance those words and images with reality, and how important it is to get the words right and put them in the right order so we do not disrupt the way of our world. Just as Confucius warned.

★ ★ ★

We have discussed some of the riddles of religion and myth, and I'll have more to say about their truth-telling in the final chapter, but I want to turn now to the riddles of science, including those in its strange (to many of us) language of mathematics. I know that some of you will throw up your hands and go quickly to the next chapter when you hear the word *mathematics*, but bear with me for a moment because I don't plan to take us very far beyond numbers. Just to infinity.

One of the challenges for all of us when it comes to mathematical storytelling is that we can't get beyond our lack of understanding of the symbols and syntax of its language—just as when we hear someone speak a language we don't understand. But the storytelling languages of mathematics made it possible for scientists to do seemingly simple things that baffled people for a long time, such as calculate the area of a circle or, to bring this closer to our modern lives, the speed of a tennis ball or a baseball.

So let me begin at the beginning with the everyday mathematics we are familiar with. It goes by the fancy name of algebra, but it starts in a simple way with numbers that are like fingers and toes, separate and singular and useful for counting things. Basic survival numbers, we might call them.

Over the years, some people have even added a religious dimension to this finger and toe business, as when the influential nineteenth-century German mathematician Leopold Kronecker said, "God made the whole numbers. All else is the work of mankind." But if we assume that God knew what he or she was doing, it's no surprise that we defer to the eminence of whole numbers and call them natural numbers, or sometimes rational numbers, not because they are reasonable but because they can include ratios of whole numbers—fractions such as ½ and ⅔.

Being by nature curious and inventive, and wanting something less easy to believe in—something to exercise our survival instinct, something more imaginative, more fantastic—mathematicians eventually came up with what they called irrational numbers, numbers such as the square root of two that could not be expressed as rational numbers. These irrationals were said to have been discovered by a Pythagorean scholar named Hippasus. However, the discovery was upsetting to his fellow Pythagoreans who, we may recall, took great pleasure not only in spheres such as the earth but also in what they considered the elegant naturalness of rational numbers. Therefore, in order to get rid of such disturbing storytelling about the irrational, they took Hippasus out to sea and threw him overboard. Or so the story goes.

But the survival of the imagination was at stake, and the trouble was only beginning. Irrational numbers survived, joined the rational clan, and together they became what were called *real numbers*—a courteous if somewhat contradictory gesture of welcome to the irrational from the mathematical imagination. However, that welcome just got the competition that always flourishes in storytelling fired up.

The game was on, and mathematicians soon came up with a new class of numbers they called transcendentals—numbers such as *pi*, the ratio of a circle's circumference to its diameter, and *e*, the basis of what became the system of logarithms.

Not surprisingly, these numbers also upset many of their mathematical colleagues. One of them, the late nineteenth-century mathematician Charles Hermite, said he "turned aside in horror from this lamentable plague" after he had—with a storyteller's pure pleasure—devised a proof of their existence so others could use transcendental numbers to tell some new stories about real world things such as the strength of earthquakes, the brightness of stars and the relationships between acid and alkaline elements in soil. These transcendental numbers also made it possible to construct a square equal in area to a given circle, something geometry could not manage. So the original naysayers swallowed their pride and put these algebraic numbers to work on other topics in the real storytelling world. New words to shape a new world.

We could say that these strange numbers represented happenings that were not happening, which is always disconcerting but in that lovely way we have seen is usually welcome to our storytelling imaginations. There were many seeming impossibilities that now became possible with these new numbers. Mathematics has always enjoyed its inspired absurdity, which may have contributed to its unpopularity even though we seem to like absurdity in other sorts of storytelling. But at the same time, the translations that mathematicians tried out with words such as *irrational* and *transcendental* have a haunting connection with classifications in our more familiar psychological and spiritual and artistic domains, with each generating its own measure of storytelling unease, and even fear.

★ ★ ★

When it comes to contradiction and uncertainty, few things match the riddle of infinity—except perhaps the riddle of divinity, with which it is often associated. Humanity is known by its dreams and its dilemmas, and the idea of infinity was a dilemma that people dreamed about and conjured with for millennia. It haunted faith keepers and theologians, philosophers and poets, scientists and many kinds of storytellers, and it nurtured riddles that still haunt us. It represented storytelling in one of its purest forms: Infinity is, one mathematician said, "a place where things happen that don't."

Like all such contradictions, infinity had troubled people and inspired storytelling for a very long time. So had the idea of the gods. Some of those who were troubled about both thought they might be able to work out a connection and take some of the mystery away from each of them. Or maybe they could share the mystery between them, they reasoned. The line between the human and the divine is notoriously hard to draw. The Greek myths—and those of many other great civilizations—are attempts to do just that. So too is the line between the finite and the infinite hard to draw. Classical, medieval and Renaissance scholars in Europe and Asia all speculated on the ways in which the mathematics of infinity might help draw that line and thereby provide insight into the divine. And in the fifteenth century, a German philosopher named Nicholas of Cusa (also called Cusanus) proposed a definition of God as "a centre which is everywhere, but whose circumference is nowhere." An image of the infinite that is also an image of the divine. Everywhere and nowhere. Someone (or something) that is and is not.

One of the first illustrations of the baffling contradictions of the infinite—defying reality even as it embraced it—was in a riddle posed 2,500 years ago by the Greek philosopher Zeno, which contained a contradiction that has haunted scientists as much as artists ever since. It went something like this: Imagine a runner setting out from A to B. First, he runs halfway to B, then half the remaining distance, then half of what's left, and so on, *ad infinitum*. That phrase means he'd have to go an infinite number of steps to cover the distance. In any given amount of time, therefore, he would never arrive. But, of course, that's the thinking of people in an ivory tower. We know from experience, from down in the yard, that he *would* arrive.

What exactly is going on here? This question kept some of the world's best mathematicians and philosophers awake for millennia. It was sometimes put in the form of a race between Achilles and a tortoise, where the speedy Achilles gives the slowpoke tortoise a head start of half the distance and then runs twice as fast. You probably know the rest. He never catches up to the tortoise, according to one impeccable line of logic involving imaginary numbers that never end. And he does catch up, according to another in the real world. Then calculus took things up, developing its own algebra of infinity with a *not happening*—an end point to those infinite steps in the race—that *is happening*.

Bob Marley, who like Ras Kumi had a genius for cutting through bafflegab, once said about money that it is just "numbers, and numbers never end." That catches the character of calculus, which draws on the riddle of infinity for its bewildering authority by insisting, with its magical mathematical wand, that the number of minutes in all time is exactly the same as the number of hours; the number of seconds the same as the number of years. The same *infinite* number. So that in the race between Achilles and the tortoise, the number of points in a mile is exactly the same as the number of points in a hundred miles. Exactly the same (infinite) number. Which neither ever reach.

Except they do reach it. That's the riddle of infinity, solvable in something called the mathematical theory of sets, which is the magical wand I just referred to and underlies the whole of calculus, giving us a way to calculate everything from the speed of a puck to the area of a hockey rink. Put as simply as I can, and in pure contradiction, calculus involves accepting that Achilles *both* catches the tortoise *and* never catches the tortoise. In mathematical terms, calculus assumes that a series of numbers like $1, \frac{1}{2}, \frac{1}{3}, \frac{1}{4}, \frac{1}{5} \ldots$ or $0, \frac{1}{2}, \frac{2}{3}, \frac{3}{4}, \frac{4}{5} \ldots$ that is approaching a limit will eventually, after an infinite number of steps, reach its limit (in these cases, 0 and 1 respectively). But such a series never *really* does, precisely because it is an *infinite* series. So calculus accepts that something both reaches its destination and never reaches it. And since that something is what calculus calculates, we have a result that both is and is not. No wonder kids the world over have trouble with the contradictions of calculus. And yet they have little cause to, for from the moment they accept that "once upon a time" means "right now," they take delight in many other contradictions.

My own interest in mathematics came from my mother, who could multiply three- and four-figure numbers together in her head and get the right answer faster than I could on a calculator. She tried to explain to me how she did it, but I had the attention span of a housefly and never learned the trick. As I got older, I understood where some of her mathematical interests and skills came from when I realized she could calculate on an abacus—an ancient counting frame developed long before our system of numbers—at what seemed to me the speed of light. It was something she learned from Chinese friends she had known from her early years in Vancouver, and some of the tricks of the calculating trade had obviously come from that. But it was her magical mental facility with large numbers that first caught my interest.

Later, a wonderfully goofy and immensely gifted high school mathematics teacher inspired me to take a degree in something called the foundation of mathematics, or pure mathematics as it was also described, which was taught at the University of British Columbia by a remarkable group of mathematicians renowned across the continent and beyond. And the marvellous and magical, bewildering and (in its contradictory way) beautiful storytelling of mathematics, filled with contradictions and uncertainties and impossibilities, nourished a curiosity about storytelling that took me to literary stories and songs, and a lifelong fascination with how storytelling works and how it helps. And then I had another gift of grace, the privilege of working for fifty years on land and sovereignty claims with Indigenous communities around the world, where stories and songs are always central. But I never put entirely to rest my uncertainty about that C-A-T. And I think it helped.

★ ★ ★

With this, I will leave mathematics, and especially calculus (I can hear sighs of relief) and turn to something more current for all of us: the uncertainties and the contradictions of what I would call civil and uncivil society, or to use terms made famous by Matthew Arnold in the middle of the nineteenth century, *Culture and Anarchy.* Arnold was not sitting on some elegant English verandah when he gave that title to his book, although its breathtaking confidence might remind us that he was living on an island. But Great Britain was anything but insular, and its future certainly not safe and secure. Arnold's country was in the midst of a deadly serious economic depression, in which differences of region and class and race were writ large, and it had just embarked on major reforms that were dividing an already deeply divided country. He—and many others—felt the menace of revolution and the disorderly forces of social, economic and political change that seemed to be sweeping the world.

It sounds grimly familiar, as similar challenges have become urgent preoccupations for many of us. And truth be told, our storytelling about it has been both a blessing and curse. The riddling question of how to balance order and disorder, civil and uncivil conduct, thoughtful and thoughtless behaviour, beauty and fear, truth and treachery is a question that continues to haunt us. It is at the centre of any act of civil disobedience and the key to any definition of terrorism. And it seems to be the fundamental challenge of our time, perhaps of all times. But let me begin with the revolutionary period of the late eighteenth century, from which we take so many of our political and professional ideas.

We met William Wordsworth earlier, describing how he was fostered alike by beauty and by fear. He lived before Arnold, but his time in revolutionary France made him a kind of fellow traveller with the Irish statesman Edmund Burke, who had been an enthusiastic supporter of the American Revolution but a fierce critic of what he saw as deliberate destruction in the French Revolution—not just the killings and class cleansings but the crushing of all convention and the poisoning of the wells of community life. "On the scheme of this barbarous philosophy," he lamented, "which is the offspring of cold hearts and muddy understandings, and which is as void of solid wisdom as it is destitute of all taste and elegance, laws are to be supported only by their own terrors, and by the concern which each individual may find in them from his own private speculations, or can spare to them from his own private interests . . . Kings will be tyrants from policy when subjects are rebels from principle. When ancient opinions and rules of life are taken away, the loss cannot possibly be estimated."

A century later, the Canadian government exerted its tyrannical power by attempting to take away the ancient opinions and rules of life of Indigenous peoples, leading to incalculable loss. But when Canada outlawed the pot-latch, a traditional gift-giving ceremony of many Indigenous nations on the West Coast that included feasting and singing and dancing as well as other forms of storytelling such as the giving of names, the Kwakwaka'wakw responded with their own stern injunction: "*Our* strict law bids *us* dance." And so they danced and celebrated. And some of them went to jail. That's the kind of resistance Burke admired. One ceremony challenging another. The fundamental act of terrorism in any political economy is one that deprives a people of their ceremonies of belief and the spiritual as well as social company they provide.

Burke was a conservative, and he was cautious about change. He was also, like Oscar Wilde, an Irishman, and a fiercely eloquent one. He identified the tension between tradition and progress that has bewildered Ireland and the rest of the world for the past couple of centuries, and he promoted a debate about what another eloquent Irishman, the critic Stephen Regan, describes as "cultural identity and political destiny, about national character and civil liberty," topics for a debate that would "establish the terms on which the future narrative of the nation [could] be constructed." Which is to say, he believed in storytelling in the service of society. The current crop of critics who talk about "narratives of nationhood" and the imaginative agencies of resistance and restitution owe more to Burke—and, I would add, to Matthew Arnold—than they would like to admit.

Burke saw the French Revolution as a kind of contagion that might spread to Ireland, which was already deeply divided along religious lines. Within a decade, he was proven right, as the Protestant Ascendancy appropriated the ideology of tradition to counter demands for progress—in the form of religious toleration and civil liberties—in an uprising of strange bedfellows (Catholic and Protestant) that was ruthlessly suppressed by the British and that set the stage for 200 years of conflict.

Burke himself was Protestant, but his mother and his wife were Catholic born, and he was a strong supporter of Catholic rights. "You are engaged in the relief of an oppressed people," he wrote proudly to his son Richard, who was an agent of the Catholic Committee in Dublin and later became leader of the Catholic Association of Ireland. Burke never finished that letter, perhaps because he didn't know how. Somewhere in his soul he saw the "terrible beauty"—in William Butler Yeats's frightening phrase—of what would become the Irish Rebellion, the Easter Rising, the Irish Civil War, and the Troubles in the north. "We cannot enjoy the rights of an uncivil and a civil state together," he argued.

Can't we? Mustn't we? The contradictions and uncertainties of doing so are an essential part of civil society, and they must be acknowledged—and some balance found—in its covenantal and constitutional storyline. In the frighteningly contemporary words of another Irish outsider, Oscar Wilde,

disobedience, in the eyes of any one who
has read history, is [our] original virtue. It is
through disobedience that progress has been
made, through disobedience and through
rebellion. Sometimes the poor are praised
for being thrifty. But to recommend thrift to
the poor is both grotesque and insulting. It
is like advising a man who is starving to eat
less. For a town or country labourer to practice thrift would be absolutely immoral. Man
should not be ready to show that he can live
like a badly fed animal . . . No: a poor man
who is ungrateful, unthrifty, discontented,
and rebellious, is probably a real personal-
ity, and has much in him. He is at any rate a
healthy protest . . . I can quite understand a
man accepting laws that protect private prop-
erty, and admit of its accumulation, as long as
he himself is able under those conditions to
realize some form of beautiful and intellectual
life. But it is almost incredible to me how a
man whose life is marred and made hideous
by such laws can possibly acquiesce in their
continuance.

Disobedience is our original virtue, nourishing storylines that embrace rather than extinguish contradiction.
Burke certainly embraced contradiction in another of his
storytelling ways, for he was the author of a great essay
at the heart of Romanticism, a period graced by contrary

souls such as William Blake, Samuel Taylor Coleridge, William Wordsworth and John Keats. Keats praised Shakespeare for his ability to maintain opposite ideas in the mind, and with his contemporaries he believed that we are all much more Shakespearean than we think when we surrender to storytelling and take pleasure in terrifying tales like Coleridge's "The Rime of the Ancient Mariner" and Blake's *Songs of Innocence and of Experience* and *The Marriage of Heaven and Hell*. In Burke's own essay "A Philosophical Enquiry into the Origin of Our Ideas of the Sublime and Beautiful" he describes dread as a possible (and radically contradictory) source of delight in the experience of what he (and his century) called the sublime. But the pleasure that terror and dread afford is only possible, Burke advised, when the threat of danger is at a certain distance. There's that "distancing" once again, full of uncertainty and contradiction. "When danger or pain press too nearly," Burke wrote, "they are incapable of giving any delight, and are simply terrible; but at certain distances, and with certain modifications, they . . . are delightful." Just as Bertolt Brecht said.

Burke's contemporaries were doing everything they could to put themselves at just the right distance to experience that contradictory delight, whether through the contemplation of death and disintegration (in graveyards and ruined abbeys and castles and revolution itself), the description of horrific scenes (of which there was no shortage in a literature that would one day inspire modern filmmaking), and the dread of divine power that Rastafarians embrace and William Blake conjures up in his poem "The Tyger." Fearful symmetry, he called it. Now that's a storytelling balance.

★ ★ ★

Annie Ned, an Athapaskan elder from Yukon territory, once said to her friend the anthropologist Julie Cruikshank, "You people talk from paper. I want to talk from Grandpa." Although the following story was given to me by my mother, Edith Cowdry, and my godmother Margaret Williams, it goes back to my grandpa's days, so maybe it will do.

Margaret was Métis, the granddaughter of a widely respected Cree woman and a Scotsman who was chief factor of the Hudson's Bay Company in Fort Qu'Appelle, Saskatchewan, during the 1880s, when Louis Riel led his people in an uprising against the new Dominion of Canada—an act of righteous disobedience that Burke and Blake and certainly Wilde would have admired.

After Riel's defeat and trial for treason (when he said he'd rather be judged bad than mad), Margaret's mother, who was eleven at the time, visited him in prison in Regina every week until his execution. How she managed this and why is a mystery (although father would probably have arranged the visits, and mother would certainly have approved of them). But however it happened, she kept a journal in which Riel—who imagined himself as the biblical psalmist David dashing down his enemies with words and music—wrote remarks such as this: "Evening prayer gives more pleasure in heaven than all the military music played by the North-West Mounted Police outside my cell window."

Margaret met my mother in Vancouver in the early years of the twentieth century, when they were both young girls about the same age as Margaret's mother had been when she visited Riel. My mother had just been called there by her father, my grandfather, from her home in Ontario where she was being raised by her aunt after her mother's death in childbirth. I can hardly imagine what it must have been like for her, travelling over two thousand miles away from the only home she'd ever known, and the only family she'd ever had, to live with a man she barely knew. But she did, and there she met Margaret, whose parents my grandfather had known from his early years living on the western plains, first in Saskatchewan and then in the foothills of Alberta.

My mother was painfully shy, at least beyond a small circle, and Margaret, like many Métis of her generation, was painfully silent about her heritage. But together they enacted a small uprising of their own. Perhaps it was inspired by Louis Riel, or by the spirit of Margaret's eleven-year-old mother, visiting him in prison until he was hanged, or by the spirit of my grandmother, who like many women displayed warrior bravery in childbirth.

Late for school one morning and arriving to find the assembly room door shut, Margaret and my mother heard the beginning of the morning hymn: "New every morning is the love / Our wakening and uprising prove."

Uprising? The two girls looked at each other. Then, without saying a word, they rose up and bolted the door. They heard another line from the hymn, "Fit us for perfect rest above," and they giggled. They giggled through the announcements and through the roll call when they were the only ones who didn't answer, "Here, ma'am."

And they were still giggling when the headmistress led the school to the assembly room door and tried to open it.

My mother would never tell me what happened next. "Use your imagination," she'd say with a smile.

In my imagination, they are still there, sitting outside the door. Like Louis Riel's uprising, theirs lasted only a short time, but their moment of defiance became mine. And it taught me that survival storytelling is often more complex than we expect. My godmother Margaret's story about her mother and Louis Riel was *her* survival story as a Métis woman. Riel's brief storyline that he wrote in her mother's journal was a celebration of *his* dignity as a righteous human being. And that adventure at the school was, I believe, more important to my eleven-year-old mother's survival as a shy young girl with a new friend in a strange town than I can easily imagine.

Resistance and Survival

Come we go burn down Babylon one more
        time . . .
Come we go chant down Babylon one more
        time . . .
For them soft! Yes, them soft! . . .
And how I know—and how I know—and that's
        how I know: . . .
With music, mek we chant down Babylon.

—Bob Marley, "Chant Down Babylon"

ONE POWERFUL IMAGE OF THE CONTRADICTIONS OF STORY-telling and its importance for survival can be found in the biblical story about Babylon, a place of exile and enslavement for the Israelites. "By the waters of Babylon we sat down and wept, when we remembered thee, O Zion" begins the song called Psalm 137—one of the psalms and evening prayers that consoled Louis Riel. "As for our harps, we hanged them up upon the trees that are therein; For they that led us away captive required of us a song, and melody in our heaviness . . . How shall we sing the Lord's song in a strange land?" How can the stranger, or the prisoner, sing of home when it seems like an impossible dream? Or sing of life when death is all around? "That's how," sings Bob Marley in his truth-tellings. And "this is how," says Louis Riel, defiantly facing execution for his uprising with the words of evening prayer. Survival is more than just being alive.

Singers and storytellers have been singing impossible songs and telling implausible stories for thousands of years. That's the spirit of "Chant Down Babylon," taking on that biblical story and making it into the story of Marley's people and their continuing exile from their home in Africa. But Marley rejects the temptation to violence, to "burn down Babylon," which is offered later in the psalm itself and instead proposes a more powerful alternative. A more permanent alternative. A storytelling alternative. That alternative is to chant it down, to sing songs of his people's spirit, and of home. To survive. "With music, mek we chant down Babylon."

Since Babylon is soft with the corruptions of material comfort, chanting *will* destroy it, sings Marley. Music is the key for his storytelling, and not just any music but *his* music, beautiful music, Jah's (Jehovah's) music—which, for Marley, is reggae.

Rastafarian storytelling—like all great traditions of story and song—is resistance storytelling. Fulfilling the Book, as he sings in his "Redemption Song." The "Book" is the King James Version of the Bible, with its Old Testament stories of resistance and survival to which Rastafarians regularly turn as they reimagine the captivity and exile of the Israelites in Egypt as the story of African enslavement in the Americas. Together they offer storytelling for survival. Stories and songs of uprising against colonial downpression. And out of this storytelling has come Rastafari, one of the great salvation and survival myths of the Americas, and of anyone who is far from their spiritual home.

And how do I know all this will work? Marley asks. "That's how," he answers. The nineteenth-century musician Robert Schumann answered a question about the meaning of a composition by playing it again. William Blake responded to a question in his poem "The Tyger" about the fearful symmetry of creation by piling on more questions. Turning to the rituals of riddle and of charm, the sponsors of song, Marley chants down Babylon. It is the *telling* of the story, the *singing* of the song, that offers freedom, more than the song or the singer. Whose spirit? The *storyteller's*.

The same can be said of the stories and songs we hear from Indigenous peoples, performed in their languages to chant down exile from their homeland in their own storytelling ceremonial sites and styles. For their storytelling, too, is about survival, about how their future is in their hands.

★ ★ ★

Often performances come unexpectedly, and so do expressions of survival. Here is one survival story by a farmer in South Africa named Piet Draghoender. It happened in the following way. Piet's ancestors, the Indigenous Khoekhoe people (once but no longer called Hottentot), had been on the move for centuries, driven from their Indigenous homeland in southwestern Africa first by Bantu-speaking Africans migrating from the north and then by white immigrants from Western Europe.

In the early 1800s, it was decided by the colonial authorities that the Kat River valley in the Eastern Cape would be an ideal place "to collect the remnants of the Hottentot race, to save them from extirpation, to civilize and Christianize them," in the words of Commissioner-General Andries Stockenström. His intentions were shaped by the language and the logic of the time, a time when Saartje Baartman, the "Hottentot Venus," was on display in salons, fairs and animal acts in London and Paris, and when "civilizing and Christianizing" Indigenous people in Canada was first being promoted.

Within a few years of their arrival in the 1820s, the pastoralist Khoekhoe surprised everyone with the success of their Kat River farming community. They had maintained their distinctive traditions of worship, having converted to Christianity some time before their removal from the Northern Cape but still calling on their shamans to perform healing ceremonies and rituals to restore the natural rhythms of the land. They fought alongside the white settlers in a series of battles against the Xhosa, and later in both World Wars, but some of them also joined with other Khoekhoe in rebellion against unscrupulous lawmakers and landowners in the 1850s. Which is to say they somehow remained themselves, even as they changed.

Then in the 1980s, over 160 years later, they were to be moved once more, all six thousand of them. This was during the last days of apartheid, when the rich farmland of the Kat River valley was wanted for white settlement. At least three government cabinet ministers came to assure the soon-to-be-displaced community that everything would be all right—even though they couldn't tell the people where they were going, or why. But the legislation was passed, the laws enforced, and within months, the Kat River community was no more.

It's an old story, except that this time there seemed to be nobody to tell it. Truth and reconciliation weren't yet the watchwords of South Africa, and many people were very scared. Others were simply too tired. But scholars were sent by the African National Congress to document the removal as best they could and to record the testimony of those who would talk.

One of them, an old man named Piet Draghoender, spoke to historian Jeff Peires from Rhodes University. Peires listened to Piet tell how his people had come to be there, and how they had made a life that was strange to them at first, coming as hunters and herders from the dry lands of the Kalahari and the Karoo. Soon this new life became the only life they could remember. Rooting themselves in the new land, they learned a new livelihood as farmers and became comfortable in a new language.

Piet was not skilled as a speaker, nor was he known as a storyteller. His eyes shifted constantly, he licked his lips nervously, he stammered and stuttered, and his hands shook uncontrollably in a field interview recorded on videotape by Peires. It is of very poor quality, probably the second or third imprint on tape that was at that time in scarce supply for the ANC. On the footage, Piet's gaunt face is visible only in relief, and his voice is blurred, intermittently break-ing up into bursts of sound. He was nearly eighty when the interview was done, an old man, frail and fussy, but he spoke to break the silence so that the history of the place wouldn't die along with its people. Survival storytelling. He answered questions, awkwardly, about the past, the present and the future of his Kat River community.

Then Peires asked, "Tell us about your neighbours, Oom [Uncle] Piet. What happened to them?"

A startled look came over Piet's face, as though he sud-denly realized the role he was playing. He stood up, and he began to speak in a quite different way, with a different rhythm, a different rhetoric and an almost delirious energy.

Here is Peires's first-hand account: "All of a sudden the tone of his speech subtly changed. From a slow hesitant beginning, he gradually worked himself up to a fever pitch, speaking like a man possessed so that it really seemed as if the frail body of the old man had become a medium of the spirit of the Kat River itself."

In literary language, Piet's outburst would be called inspired, in a tradition of lament that was both his own and as old as humankind. It is from the Bible, and it is from the long tradition of southern African praise songs. It is from ancient Greek elegies, and from the chants of mourners in modern India. It is a tradition in which we speak with a knowledge that is not necessarily ours, of events that some-times have not yet happened, as though we had seen it all before and yet are as astonished as if it were happening for the first time. And in this case it was a performance, deliv-ered in a farmer's field in the Eastern Cape of South Africa, which can be seen and heard only second-hand on a hopelessly poor videotape.

However, in the short time since it was recorded, Piet Draghoender's lament has become a notable part of southern African literature, its place secured by the literary historian Michael Chapman when he published and placed it front and centre in his classic study, *Southern African Literatures*. Anyone trying to determine exactly what happened in the Kat River valley wouldn't be helped much by Piet's lament and might well be put off by the notion that Piet was a man possessed by the spirit of the place. And yet his testimony rings true not because he seems like an honest man—which he does, his apparent honesty enhanced by his awkward performance—but because it is certified by a tradition of lament that is universal and sadly familiar. Here is part of Piet Draghoender's lament.

> what is
> what is he
> yes! Mr. Stockenstroom
>
> so I feel very heartsore
> these wars
> my father has stood for a war
> my grandfather has stood for a war
> my children
> my father's children
> have stood for a war
>
> to make this place free

the Lord will not allow you to be
taken so
and be thrown away
and that and that be given away
from from from the Lord for for
for the enemy's
put it in that pigsty
put it in the pigsty
for it belongs to nothing
what is
what is he?

This was the music of what happened, a song of protest and an evening prayer. Louis Riel would have understood. So can we all.

★ ★ ★

"None but ourselves can free our minds," sang Bob Marley, echoing the words of the Jamaican prophet Marcus Garvey in a speech he gave at Liberty Hall in Nova Scotia in 1937. In this sense, all songs and stories can be resistance songs, for when they are true and believable they are much more than simple protests. They cross boundaries without losing a sense of place, and they generate confidence to live in the wider world to which we all in some sense belong.

When the Doukhobors came to Canada from persecution in Russia in the 1890s, with moral and financial encouragement from Leo Tolstoy, they brought with them a spirit of defiance and a determination to maintain a community that was steeped in spiritual orderings. "Spirit wrestler" was the original (and originally unfriendly) meaning of the word *Doukhobor*. When they got here, they were offended by Canadian authority—not because it was particularly oppressive but because it was generally secular. The government earned their disdain, as governments often do, by insisting the Doukhobors do, and not do, certain things. When they refused, there was violent resistance from a radical group within the community. In retaliation the government imprisoned some of the brethren and took many of the Doukhobor children away to school to be indoctrinated into the secular world of "civilized" indulgence that their people had suffered for centuries to avoid.

But wise people in the Doukhobor community knew that chanting down Babylon was a more righteous and ultimately a more radical response to the government orders, and a group of Doukhobor women made the very long walk of protest from the interior of British Columbia down to Vancouver's Victory Square, which was a memorial to those who died in the First World War, where they sat down and set up camp. I remember going down to hear them singing psalms in the evenings. I have seldom heard music as sweet, or as soulful—music that uniquely blended solo and choral melodies with unison singing in octaves. "The singing of psalms is like honey," they said, adding that if they were ever to stop singing they would cease being a people. With those songs, and their celebration of the values of their community, they sang their way into a society that has been made much better by their presence.

★ ★ ★

I came to literature, as many of us do, by way of songs, with bedtime rhymes and riddles preparing me both for hymns in church and for the rhythms of rock and roll. Popular songs of my parents' choosing and then of my own made me aware of the complicated and contradictory hold such songs have on us. Folk songs, mostly from the Americas and the British Isles, shaped my life in the 1960s. Many of those songs were from the extraordinary treasury of albums put out by Moses Asch through his label, Folkways Records. Bob Marley's *Catch a Fire* caught me up in the 1970s, U2's *Joshua Tree* in the 1980s, and Gordon Lightfoot and Ian Tyson and Buffy Sainte-Marie and Joni Mitchell and Stan Rogers and Neil Young and many others have been with me before and since. All of them offered storytelling that was rare and precious: a sense of community and a promise of hope.

But the ones that overwhelmed me were survival songs, such as the deeply moving memorial for those who lost their lives in a 1958 mine disaster in Nova Scotia. Called "The Ballad of Springhill," it was written and first sung by Peggy Seeger (Pete's half-sister) and British folksinger Ewan MacColl and includes a couple of haunting lines from one of the miners, all of whom were experienced enough to know that they had only a slim chance of survival. But for them, singing offered a better alternative than succumbing to despair. "We're out of light and water and bread," they sang, "so we'll live on song and hope instead." Hope and the promise—or just the possibility—of balance. Survival storytelling.

Sometimes it's not the song itself, but the singing. Just as sometimes it's not the storyline, but the storytelling.

★ ★ ★

The anthropologist Bronislaw Malinowski used to talk about what he called the "weirdness coefficient" of magic. I have always taken that to include the magic of song. For to me, it was weird how some sad songs made me feel happy, some scary songs made me feel safe, and many of the loveliest songs made me cry. This matched the contradictions of my life, with feelings of insecurity completely at odds with good fortune in family and friends. Eventually, I realized that songs kept me company. And yet these kinds of contrary reactions to some of them kept surprising me.

It *still* surprises me that we understand right away when Kris Kristofferson tells us that feeling good was easy for him when he listened to Bobby McGee sing the blues on their road trip across the country. Or when Elton John reminds us in "Sad Songs (Say So Much)" that when we are feeling hopeless it is often a contradictory comfort of sad songs that can help, not only by keeping us company but by saying things in a gentle way. And it still surprises me that during desperately difficult times—such as the social and economic depression and the devastating climate changes experienced during the 1930s on the great plains and prairies of the Americas, with dust storms and family distress and homeless despair affecting almost everyone in some way, mass migration underway around the world, and a host of diseases taking a toll following the disaster of the

Spanish flu a decade earlier—that people turned to songs to help them through. Often very sad songs. Across Canada and the United States people were losing their farms and their families, but the songs that gave them courage to live another day were well acquainted with the grief they were experiencing. These were songs that embraced the sorrow and suffering that was gripping everyone, and yet somehow gave them hope. These were their survival songs, even though many of the singers knew they were not likely to survive. However you understand it, that's weird.

But it was also widespread, for many of the sufferers listened happily to songs written and sung by blue yodeller Jimmie Rodgers. It was said that a typical weekly shopping list for a southern American family on the edge of destitution during the Dirty Thirties was a pound of butter, a slab of bacon, a sack of flour, and the latest Jimmie Rodgers record. They all knew he was dying of tuberculosis. And they all knew that many of them were too.

> When it rained down sorrow,
> It rained all over me . . .
> I've been fighting like a lion,
> Looks like I'm going to lose
> 'Cause there ain't nobody
> Ever whipped the T.B. blues

Or maybe it was Hank Williams, lamenting that he's

> never seen a night so long
> And time goes crawling by

The moon just went behind the clouds
To hide its face and cry

Did you ever see a robin weep
When leaves begin to die?
Like me, he's lost the will to live
I'm so lonesome, I could cry

Or perhaps a song like "Irene, Goodnight," written and sung by Leadbelly:

Sometimes I live in the country
Sometimes I live in town.
Sometimes I take a great notion
To jump in the river and drown

There are versions of such songs everywhere, all over the world and from time immemorial. They are songs that put you back together by telling you what it's like to be broken apart. Songs that mirror the magic of Charlie Chaplin, making "a grail of laughter of an empty ash can" (in the words of the American poet Hart Crane). Songs in which the contradictions we have seen to be inherent in all storytelling kick in loudly and, in another weird contradiction, lovingly. Songs that surrender to the mystery of forces beyond human understanding, rather than promising mastery over them. How this happens, how a kind of joy comes out of a song or story of sorrow, is one of the mysteries of art and of life, as baffling as any of the mysteries of science. It is an amazing grace, if only for a moment or two before we turn to worry about something else, or, if we are young, to fall asleep. It gives us the balance we sometimes need to get through another day. And the only way it works is if we believe in it. We know how to do this, for we have been doing it all our lives. And when asked how they make this magic, good singers and storytellers say, "That's how."

* * *

The anthropologist Michael Asch, whom I first met when he was working with the Dene in the Northwest Territories and I was working with Thomas Berger on the Mackenzie Valley Pipeline Inquiry, tells a story that takes us further into this magical mystery. Michael's father was Moses Asch, the founder of Folkways Records, who recorded many of the great singers and songwriters of the twentieth century from all over the world—a legacy of song and spoken word for which Michael arranged the inspired stewardship of Smithsonian/Folkways Recordings after his father died.

Michael recalled for me a kitchen-table conversation at their New York house between Bob Dylan and Pete Seeger. Dylan was playing a new song he had written, with a series of impossible questions reminiscent of William Blake's poem "The Tyger" and their inscrutable answers just blowing in the wind. Seeger, notorious both for his patience and his impatience, immediately took issue with the sentiment, arguing that those answers were to be found in the hearts of men and women, *not* blowing in the wind.

Was this a conflict between innocence and experience? Or between fate and freedom, written for modern times? Or between reality and the imagination, the staple of stories and song? Or between acceptance and defiance? And do we need to take sides? Although none of these contraries are exclusively poetic or philosophic, all are deeply political. Yet—and this is the conclusion both Seeger and Dylan reached in their songwriting, if not around the kitchen table—each mirrors the other. We know reality only through our imaginations, as Oscar Wilde argued. Freedom may just be an upscale word for nothing left to lose as Kris Kristofferson sang, but that could also mean simply waiting until fate makes its play. A great code can be something to be interpreted, like scripture or song or certain natural phenomena—but it can also be something to be obeyed, like a genetic code or a binding covenant or the weather. And a blowing wind can be a lot like a breath of inspiration or the immanent spirit.

But what about some of the even more fundamental questions that trouble us. Questions such as "Why did my friend get sick?" or "Why is there so much suffering in the world?" or "How much is enough?" Stories and songs may help us resist despair by offering new ways of dealing with the old answer, "We don't know." For we still hope for *answers* from storytelling, and for an escape from the loneliness and the loss, the bewilderment and the despair, that reality imposes on us. And an answer often isn't there. Expecting comfort from a bunch of words "is like telling mourners round the graveside about resurrection. They want the dead back," said the West Indian poet Derek Walcott. But then another poet storyteller pushes defiantly back against reality, resisting it even while surrendering to it. "Do not stand at my grave and weep, / I am not there. I do not sleep. / I am a thousand winds that blow. / I am the diamond glints on snow. / I am the sunlight on ripened grain. / I am the gentle autumn rain" is the beginning of the poem "Immortality," believed to be written in 1934 by Clare Harner, which was famously read on the BBC in 1995 by the father of a soldier killed by a bomb in Northern Ireland. Resistance and defiance for survival.

During the 1970s, I listened to a young Argentinian tell about the mothers of the disappeared in his homeland, and how they gather into three groups: One group asked for the names of the disappeared to be known and remembered. Another group wanted the bodies of the deceased back, so they could be buried in a proper ceremony. I have heard similar laments by Indigenous people from central Australia to southern Africa and from Kamloops to Kenora, and they all need to be heard. We need to bury our dead. But it was the third group of mothers whose cry was itself a song. They wanted the dead back, *alive again*. That was their unequivocal claim on the past, and on reality. And it is completely without irony. They want the imagination to change the world, to make night into day, to make silence into song. It is a wish, full of faith, that resonates in the heart of anyone who has lost a loved one, or lost their way, or had it stolen from them. They are living in hope for something they *know* is hopeless. But they also know that such knowledge is as uncertain as anything else. So they keep on hoping. The residential schools tried to destroy hope for Indigenous people. They were out of light and water and bread and had nothing left to live on except songs and stories and hope.

Storytelling kept hope alive. Defiance and determination kept those who survived alive.

I think of a poem by Thomas Hardy about the oxen in stables everywhere that kneel at Christmas in memory of the ox that is said to have kneeled in the manger when Jesus was born. It's storytelling time, once-upon-a-time-is-right-now time.

Christmas Eve, and twelve of the clock.
"Now they are all on their knees,"
An elder said as we sat in a flock
By the embers in hearthside ease.

We pictured the meek mild creatures where
They dwelt in their strawy pen,
Nor did it occur to one of us there
To doubt they were kneeling then.

So fair a fancy few would weave
In these years! Yet, I feel,
If someone said on Christmas Eve,
"Come; see the oxen kneel,

"In the lonely barton by yonder coomb
Our childhood used to know,"
I should go with him in the gloom,
Hoping it might be so.

★ ★ ★

People all over the world read the Bible and the Qur'an, recite prayers to household gods and heavenly spirits, call out and cry out, sing songs of freedom and read stories of revolution or medical remedy. Hoping it might, or might not, be so. And hoping they can balance the possibility of a better future with what seems like the prospect of everlasting despair. This attempt at balance is what William Wordsworth was calling for, and hoping for, when he lamented how in his time of troubles (a time in many ways not unlike ours), "a multitude of causes . . . [were] acting with a combined force to blunt the discriminating powers of the mind, and unfitting it for all voluntary exertion to reduce it to a state of almost savage torpor." It's a terrifying phrase. Savage torpor. Brutal surrender. Stupefied, numb despair. It is where we all find ourselves sometimes in our lives, and it is a state from which we always need relief. Something to give us ease in the midst of so much disease—social and economic and political and medical. And we need some assistance in finding that relief. That's where storytelling can help us, bringing a sliver of light, a spirit of defiance, and some pleasure into the sometimes sunless and dispiriting workplace of life and giving us direction and encouragement.

In times of crisis, when we feel as if we are in the fog amid the fury of wind and wave, we know the liturgy by heart. And whatever it is we wish for—peace, or love, or health, or happiness, or a safe harbour—we hope with all our hearts and all our minds that it will somehow come to pass. If we are fortunate, we can turn to the comfort of family and friends and our communities, calling out and hoping. That hope, held dear in all forms of storytelling, represents a competition with reality and a defiance of the inevitable or the already apparent.

★ ★ ★

Whatever enlarges hope inspires courage. Survival stories of all kinds are worldwide. And often they surprise us, as Piet's surprised even himself. I remember another, with a more cheerful cast, from close to home in British Columbia. It was a story that we heard about in Chapter Two, performed rather than printed, in the territory of the Gitxsan people who have lived in what is now British Columbia along the Skeena River for thousands of years, and whose survival to the present offers an inspiring history of determination and dignity and responsible stewardship of their homeland. One of their most distinguished elders was Neil Sterritt, who led the community in a recognition of their ancient residence and modern sovereignty in their homeland. The resulting Supreme Court decision established both a legal and a constitutional storyline (which has since been reinforced by other Supreme Court decisions) for Indigenous sovereignty in Canada.

That was good news. But Neil's work, like Canada's relationship with Indigenous people, was unfinished. He had a storyteller's gift for surprise, which he used on one occasion to protect the traditional hunting and fishing in his people's territory—traditions that included spiritual and legal and constitutional responsibilities for stewardship that are central to his people's identity. The story he offered about this centrality displays an inspired bit of mischief.

Exasperated by decades of aggravation and increasingly frequent arrests, Neil announced that the community would be fishing at a particular time and place prohibited by government regulations but sanctioned by centuries of Gitxsan practice and by healthy fish stocks. The police, along with a large contingent of officials from the department of fisheries, arrived in force and ready for trouble. But they were stopped short by a blockade organized in what Neil mischievously described to me as "traditional" Gitxsan battle order: children in front; women next, the guardians of place; and the men hiding safely behind, urging everyone on. On a signal from Neil, the fishers set out their traps and nets and lines. The assembled settler "authorities" demanded the people move. But the Gitxsan, who had their own spiritual as well as constitutional mandate, refused.

A classic stand-off. Then, while the fishers began their fishing, the government agents moved menacingly forward, closer and closer to the blockade. At another signal, the children reached into the little bags they were carrying, pulled out some mysterious missiles—and threw a volley of marshmallows at the advancing forces.

Startled and scared—after all, they were in Gitxsan territory and the Gitxsan are a famously determined people—the police and government officers covered their heads, turned their backs and ran for cover. Their embarrassing retreat from the marshmallow attack by the child warriors was caught on camera by the very large media contingent that Neil had invited along. You could almost hear the laughter all the way to Vancouver. The story and, most embarrassingly, the images made the evening news and newspaper headlines throughout the west, and the confrontation became known locally as the Marshmallow War. There was no question who won, and not just that day. The confrontation prompted the government to negotiate a responsible agreement with the Gitxsan, and it inspired many other Indigenous peoples across the country to use civil disobedience and defiance to assert their rights and to establish the principle that understanding colonial history and Indigenous heritage offers the only way forward.

"Together Today for Our Children Tomorrow" was the name given by the Council for Yukon Indians to the land claim they presented to the federal government in 1973, signalling the beginning of a new era in relationships between First Nations and the nation of Canada, and the principles upon which it must be founded: that Indigenous children must win not only the local battles but the 500-year war against their people; that ignorance and stupidity—not police or politicians or public servants—are the real problem; and that nurturing truth and belief with good storytelling can help us move towards reconciliation.

★ ★ ★

I want to turn now to a poem that offers another kind of survival storyline for another kind of challenge, one that has almost universal currency not just in Canada but around the world. But first a digression about poems and songs, since this poem, like so many others, has some of the features of song and is called a *lyric* poem, a name that comes from a stringed musical instrument that has been around for thousands of years. The lyre has often been used to symbolize an ancient conflict that has defined many communities and entire civilizations—a conflict, or more truly a competition, between the musical lyre and the hunting bow, the dreamer and the doer. It is a measure of their importance for human survival that for millennia the musician and the storyteller have been accorded power comparable to that of the warrior and the worker.

This poem tells a powerful story, a very human story. In the very early days of storytelling around the world, poems and songs were among storytelling's most popular forms, with ballads and epics being favoured (often with musical accompaniment, just like our musicals), and with rhyming (one of Chaucer's favourite techniques) and riddling (especially in very early English poetry) to maintain interest. They were part of the storyteller's toolkit.

There was solid strategy here, for storytellers often performed to audiences busy eating and drinking and talking and maybe even dancing. Storytelling with spellbinding rhymes and robust rhythms would help engage audiences by offering that special kind of storytelling fun that we first take up as children—the fun that parents often use to enliven what used to be called cautionary tales, and that now holds us close to the games and stories many of us enjoy on our smartphones and tablets. The Latin word for song was *carmen*, which is where we get our English word *charm*, and the charm of a good song—and a good poem—is ultimately inseparable from its storytelling style. And although we are often hesitant to admit this, it is very often style as much as substance that makes us believe what we see or hear.

When I taught poetry, I would tell my students at the beginning of the year that we were going to memorize some poems. Always there were groans of distress. So I would then ask how many songs they knew by heart. Forty or fifty was the average. And as we talked about their songs, it became clear that they were completely comfortable, in their minds as well as their hearts, with being uncertain about their meaning. For them, the meaning of songs was a silly distraction, as silly as the idea of beauty. For them, the songs they liked were simply *good* songs; telling good, although certainly not always happy, stories. And most importantly, the songs were good for them, giving them pleasure even if they were not quite sure why. They just knew these songs helped them sort out and manage the conflicts and contradictions and uncertainties of their lives by surrounding them with riddling challenges and charms. Without exaggeration, they felt that these songs sometimes saved their lives. They believed those songs were there for them, and happily defied the incomprehensible lyrics and inconsistent storylines of the songs by surrendering to their rhythms and melodies. They surrendered to the storytelling of song.

But let's get back to that poem. The author called it an ode, a kind of praise song, to a bird—in this case a nightingale—singing a sweet song. Put that way, the poem sounds trivial, but if so, the nightingale's song is trivial in the way some of those songs my students and my children loved sometimes seemed trivial to their teachers and parents. But for this poet, the nightingale's song helped him make it through the night. No small thing for him, as you will understand when you hear the state that he was in. For this storytelling poem is about someone in despair, and the momentary comfort the song of the nightingale offered him. And about the way that moment became a memory and gave him courage to keep on living another day.

The poem was written over 200 years ago by a young man named John Keats, who, instead of going into medicine for which he had been trained, turned to the discipline of storytelling in poetry and took it as seriously as any scientist takes their vocation. The poem's opening words are "My heart aches." Three thumping words—in what has become, or maybe always has been, a predictable and often permanent opener for young and old alike. "My . . . heart . . . aches." A bit melodramatic maybe, but so are we all sometimes. However we take it, this early-nineteenth-century poet is not in a good way. And he *was* a young man, but one who knew his life was almost over. For he had tuberculosis, very often deadly at the time—a time when what he called "the weariness, the fever and the fret" were a common lot, uncomfortably like our own times.

For this poet, his failing health was both very personal and seemingly universal, again much like our time with the pandemic and the plague of insecurities and inequities and injustices it has highlighted. Keats lived in a time and a place where people both old and young "sit and hear each other groan; / Where palsy shakes a few sad, last grey hairs, / Where youth grows pale, and spectre-thin, and dies." You can hear failing health in the rhythms of that last line— beginning with three beats, "youth grows pale"; then two, "spectre thin"; and a final one, "dies." Keats not only had a bad cough, he had just buried his brother, who had followed their mother to the grave with tuberculosis. Keats knew the rhythm and melody of death as well as of life. And he knew he would follow soon. No wonder for him it was a time and a place "where but to think is to be full of sorrow / And leaden-eyed despairs." It doesn't sound as if the story is going to end well. But stories specialize in surprises.

Meanwhile, the poet contemplates various kinds of escape: into booze, "that [he] might drink, and leave the world unseen" or into opioids (opium was the drug of choice back then, available at low cost from the local corner store). And he also knows about the temporary liberation of getaway stories and seductive songs. But instead he contemplates the ultimate escape, suicide. "For many a time / I have been half in love with easeful Death, / Call'd him soft names in many a mused rhyme, / To take into the air my quiet breath; / Now more than ever seems it rich to die, / To cease upon the midnight with no pain."

And then the song of a nightingale saves him . . . at least for today. Remember that word. *Today*. The nightingale's song saves him by its beauty, and what we might also call the truth of that beauty, for both truth and beauty defy definition. It saves him by surprising him at just the right moment—a reminder how important surprise can be in storytelling. And he is saved by the thought that a song like this might have been heard "in ancient days by emperor and clown," which is to say, by anyone, anyone who needs help.

In particular, he imagines Ruth from the biblical story of the woman from Moab. Ruth married an Israelite, from a country to the west of Moab with which the Moabites were often in conflict; and together they came to live in Ruth's homeland. But after her husband's early death, Ruth went back to Israel, where her mother-in-law, Naomi, would be safe in her homeland but where Ruth was an unwelcome and impoverished stranger who had to go to work in the farm fields to support them both. And John Keats imagines that the nightingale's song might once have "found a path / Through the sad heart of Ruth, when, sick for home, / She stood in tears amid the alien corn." Her tears become his, too, and suddenly the poet is not alone, even across millennia. His imagination brings him into Ruth's company, and reality gives him the beauty of the nightingale's song, and together they save him from despair and the dangerous fear it brought him. In turn, *his* song helps *us* across the centuries, ringing as true today as it did back then, offering comfort and consolation and company. And we don't even have to memorize it.

Recalling "Ode to a Nightingale," it is no surprise to me that U2's "I Still Haven't Found What I'm Looking For" has had such a following. With its opening drumming (which always reminds me of Keats's opening lines) and its cry of despair, that song Bono sings is a prayer—a prayer signalling what the seventeenth-century poet George Herbert called "a heart in pilgrimage," a prayer that is in all our hearts if we let ourselves go walkabout in the company of stories and songs. Such company won't necessarily lift us out of ourselves or offer us an escape from reality. But it can bring us *into* ourselves, however scary that may be, and open reality up to our imaginations.

Sometimes the way to handle our sense of fear and foreboding is to *tell* a story. Our own scary story. My daughter Sarah works at the Centre for Addiction and Mental Health (CAMH) in Toronto—a place that has recognized the importance of community for nourishing hope and mental health by establishing a sweat lodge, a sacred fire, and a medicine garden in a ceremonial healing space for Indigenous patients. The centre has also recognized the importance of stories to connect and heal us. Sarah is leading a campaign that chose the simple watchwords "Not Suicide. Not Today." It is accompanied by a series of stories told by survivors from all walks of life, all with the same message: Tell your story. Tell it to someone. Right now. *Today*. Before it's too late. We hope other people's stories will inspire you, but the one story that matters and that can save you is yours. And you are its most important storyteller. By telling your story to someone, you create a community, however small. You are not alone any longer. And even if nobody is near, somebody from a story, like the biblical Ruth, can offer company until you find someone to listen to *your* story. And you will.

★ ★ ★

I want to close this chapter with another story, one that comes down to a few words—words that helped people suffering from the kind of despair, the "savage torpor," that Wordsworth talked about. A despair that is experienced by many people these days, for many reasons.

Storytelling in whatever form—words and images, melodies and rhythms—provides a declaration of our independence from the tyranny of the everyday, offering a first line of defence against the chaotic confusions of the world and giving us dignity amidst the fierce and often fatal indecencies of life. Storytelling provides a way of managing life and death, the joy and sadness of love, the mysteries of friendship and contentment and the menace of accidents and disease. And even if we understand some of these things a little better now than we did during the last ice age, the ancient and universal impulse to turn to stories and songs to embrace ourselves is still with us.

Listen to the hopeful advice of the Uruguayan writer Eduardo Galeano, reminding us to keep an open heart and mind for apparently unlikely stories and unexpected outcomes.

> The literature that is most political, most
> deeply committed to the political process of
> change, can be the one that least needs to
> name its politics, in the same sense that the
> crudest political violence is not necessarily
> demonstrated by bombs and gunshots . . .
> Those who approach the people as if they
> were hard of hearing and incapable of imagin-
> ation confirm the image of them cultivated by
> their oppressors . . . Literature that shrinks
> the soul instead of expanding it, as much as it
> might call itself militant, objectively speaking
> is serving a social order, which daily nibbles
> away at the variety and richness of the human
> condition . . . I believe that literature can

recover a political, revolutionary path every
time it contributes to the revelation of reality . . . From this point of view, a love poem
can be more fertile than a novel dealing with
the exploitation of miners in the tin mines or
workers on the banana plantations.

The geography of things that unsettle us or disorient
us or fill us with dread is never all that clear, and that is
one of the things that make them scary—that, and the fact
that they sometimes seem to come from within ourselves,
which makes them even scarier. And yet, a story or a song
or a proverb or a prayer can offer ways of dealing with such
things by simply *naming* them. The following story can be
told in three or four words, and those words have helped
many people. Here it is.

Some years ago, I was in Saskatoon for a gathering
of mostly Indigenous men and women to talk about stories and the help and hope they can provide to those who
were suffering from a variety of substance and domestic
abuses, much of it the legacy of residential schools. This
gathering was over twenty-five years ago, before our Royal
Commission on Aboriginal Peoples and our Truth and
Reconciliation Commission, when there was little help
available to—and often little sympathy for—those who were
struggling. Struggling to stay alive and struggling to find a
reason to want to.

One of the speakers that afternoon was Eduardo·
Duran, trained in both traditional Indigenous healing and
Western psychological therapy techniques. He described

the situation of many of the Navajo people he was working with: They were physically and mentally very ill, and most were not going to get well in any conventional sense, or live much longer, and they knew it. But he wanted to give them a reason to live as long as they could, and some relief in this last phase of their life.

He struggled with all the techniques he could think of from both traditions of medicine, and none of them seemed to help. And then slowly he began to realize that although their illnesses were both mental and physical, their condition was spiritual. We can agree or disagree with his diagnosis, but his insight saved his patients. As he told the story, it became clear that it saved him, too, from despair. Even more importantly, as he obviously hoped, it saved many of those in his audience that afternoon.

In his medical diagnosis, Duran had thought about spiritual traditions from both Indigenous and Western cultures. This process was complicated, because Christianity had sponsored much of the suffering that the people he was working with had experienced, and it had eroded their traditional faith. But Christianity had also drawn many of them into a sense of community. Within that companionship, traditional ceremonies had not all been silenced. Ceremonies such as the Sun Dance were still practised in a summer ritual by most of the Indigenous nations on the western plains when the berries were ripening. Duran recognized in both Christianity and the Sun Dance a central story of sacrificial suffering, specifically the crucifixion of Christ and the heroic self-mutilation by certain warriors that was once a Sun Dance ritual, in both cases to secure the survival of their people. And he turned this realization into a celebration—one as contradictory and as uncertain as the spiritual often is—of what he called "the sacredness of suffering." That phrase alone, he said, had been immediately embraced by the men and women he was working with, and its spirit transformed what for many of them were relatively short but—insofar as the word does not seem ironic at their expense—happy lives. It did not heal them but it helped them. Just as it helped many in his audience that day.

The sacredness of suffering. It's a phrase that brings stories and histories into a new kind of communion, a new kind of balance. It's an unforgettable, contradictory, uncertain, ceremonial phrase. And it's a phrase I have never forgotten.

Competition, Conflict and Collaboration

"I've got a better one."

—ǂKhomani elder Andries Olyn
responding to a story by Khoekhoe
storyteller Levi Namaseb in South Africa

I HAD GONE TO THE KALAHARI DESERT IN THE NORTHERN CAPE of South Africa in the mid-1990s to listen to San (Bushman) storytelling, and there I had the rare privilege of listening to many traditional storytellers from the ǂKhomani community, most of whom were quite old. They told their stories and sang their songs in their Indigenous language about the spiritual and material life of a desert homeland they had shared with springbok and gemsbok and lions and leopards and a variety of nutritional plants whose roots provided medicinal resources—a homeland they had shared, that is, until they were thrown out sixty years earlier to "make room" for a national park. They also told stories about ancestral spirits and imaginary creatures not part of the imaginative world of European and settler African storytelling, but as unsettling as anything by the brothers Grimm. The stories were always performed, since their language (from the Khoisan family) has five clicks and eight tones and at that time did not have a written form.

I was fortunate to have with me Levi Namaseb, a friend and colleague and distinguished southern African linguist from Namibia. His native language, Khoekhoe (one of eight that he speaks), is also part of the Khoisan family, and he had inherited from his mother, a legendary storyteller, a gift for both language and storytelling. We were welcomed by the ‡Khomani, and by some gift of grace we first met a family of elderly sisters—|Una Rooi, Kais Brau, |Abaka Koper—and their cousin Griet Bott, who had somehow kept together over the past sixty years and still spoke their language (now in the keeping of a few elderly speakers, but of increasing interest to the young). They told us stories and sang songs with the energy and enthusiasm of much younger storytellers, taking us home to the desert and to their families and away from their difficult lives in impoverished townships where tuberculosis and many other troubles were endemic. But their memories of their desert homeland were as fresh as yesterday's events, and their spirits as sturdy and as full of mischief as the stories they told.

After spending a good deal of time with the sisters, we asked about other storytelling survivors from their community, which had been scattered throughout the Northern Cape. They immediately suggested an elder named Andries

Olyn, who they said was a wonderful storyteller. So Levi and I went to meet him.

We arrived at his small farmstead one late afternoon and were received with courteous formality. After tea and cookies and cordial conversation, we asked if he would tell us some stories. He said, firmly, that he didn't know any. We expressed our surprise and disappointment, but he was implacable. So Levi took up the challenge, and for the next ten minutes he encouraged Andries, flattering him with the comments of the other community elders that had sent us on this visit. He even gently mocked him. "A famous storyteller without any stories?" he asked mischievously. He tried everything, but to no avail.

Finally, with a storyteller's sure instinct, he thanked him for his hospitality and said that as a gesture of gratitude, he would tell a story himself. Which he did. With stunning verbal pyrotechnics and spectacular hand and body impressions, Levi performed a cautionary tale about an ogre, full of scary suspense and surprises both dreadful and delightful.

As soon as Levi had finished, our host said "I've got a better one." And Andries and Levi began telling stories, back and forth, for the next three hours until well after dark. Scheherazade couldn't have done any better, and the lives of Andries and Levi didn't even depend on it. But maybe they did.

"I've got a better one" is a storytelling challenge that has echoed throughout the ages in every culture in the world, and it's probably where what we now think of as storytelling began. In ancient Greece, literary critics were the judges appointed to decide between rival rhapsodists—the rappers, or epic storytellers, of their day. And while sports provided other entertainment in what we call the Eurasian classical world, they also provided a pattern for storytelling competitions and other oral performances. Indeed, many of the terms of what we now call rhetoric came to European languages from the foot race and the wrestling mat.

But that afternoon and evening I witnessed something special: a competition between two storytellers from southern Africa speaking in their own languages and storytelling traditions, with the truth of their stories inseparable from the ceremonial spell of their storytelling. Here was a modern celebration of an ancient tradition of storytelling in a cave in the mountains or a clearing in the forest or a waterhole in the desert or a strand by the ocean shore. And here was storytelling to balance the powers of the human imagination and the wonders of the world. And to give pleasure.

★ ★ ★

I mentioned that the ‡Khomani language did not have a written form, although one would soon be created for them by Levi, who had some years earlier done the same for his native Khoekhoe speech. But at that time, their commitment to oral performance was also complicated by a competition between orality and literacy that has a long and troublesome history in the relationship between Indigenous peoples and settler societies. These days this competition between orality and writing often bedevils the dynamics of tribunals and courts in which land and sovereignty claims are addressed, though the popularity of performance, enhanced by new virtual technology, is changing this. All that's needed now is to learn how to listen as diligently as we learn how to read.

Until all too recently, Indigenous oral storytelling about history and homeland has been discounted as unreliable—not verifiable and therefore not "true" in the way written documents are, even when the storytelling is performed by elders as scrupulously trained in testimonial storytelling as any academic scholar or religious faith keeper, and even when their truth is verified by a select group of other elders—who must be in attendance in a certain storytelling place, often wearing certain ceremonial regalia, for both the storytellers *and* their stories to be believed. Such storytellers are custodians of the truth and the beauty of their heritage. And they keep alive an ancient competition between oral and written storytelling and between images and words.

Now I certainly do not dispute the benefits of literacy, especially after the invention of printing in our industrialized world. But the marginalization of those who do not have a written form of their spoken language often involves more than what literate society perceives as a linguistic disadvantage, for it ignores the many forms of writing in non-syllabic and non-alphabetic forms such as the pictographic and petroglyphic images of Indigenous cultures, north and south, and the condolence canes and wampum belts of the Iroquois nations, the carving of totem poles and masks and the cedar bark baskets and hats and the woven blankets and robes of many West Coast nations—only a few of the many forms of "writing without words" that Indigenous peoples around the world have used.

These forms of writing without words are definitive. They make meaning. And they tell stories. They also remind us that sign systems of all kinds can be both beautiful *and* true and have been with us for a very long time, probably since language itself began. And the distinction between orality and literacy is not as simple as we sometimes assume. For the central institutions of our so-called written cultures—our churches and temples and mosques, our courts and parliaments and congresses, and our schools—are themselves defined by oral traditions with strict ceremonial protocols and conventions.

But this realization does not seem to have made its way into the sophisticated minds of those, especially those in these same institutions, who have sponsored a brutally prejudicial and absolutely false interpretation that those who do not have spoken-word writing are somehow stalled in an early stage of human development. Primitive. Many so-called experts in cognitive development have insisted that the writing of spoken languages marked an evolutionary "advance" that set Us apart from Them, and saved Us from what Marshall McLuhan (who should have known better) called a "return to the Africa within" us.

Writing frees the mind for original, abstract thought, some say. The eye analyzes, the ear tribalizes, chimed in McLuhan. Other advocates of this human intellectual "progress" added a list of additional limitations: oral cultures are imprisoned in the present, uninterested in definitions, unable to make analytic distinctions, incapable of separating knowledge itself from the process of knowing, and incorrigibly totalizing. Oral cultures understand the

world in magical rather than scientific terms, some com-
mentators still insist, and those in such cultures who have
any acquaintance whatsoever with writing are agonizingly
aware of the "vast complex of powers forever inaccessible
without literacy," and realize that literacy "is absolutely
necessary for the development not only of science but
also of history, philosophy, explicative understanding of
literature and of any art, and indeed for the explanation
of language itself." This last catalogue of handicaps is
from a book by Walter Ong titled *Orality and Literacy: The
Technologizing of the Word*, which became a primer for the
competition between orality and literacy and fuelled the
conflict I have been describing with Indigenous peoples
around the world.

One further thing that gets forgotten in this outpour-
ing of insults is that another kind of sophisticated "reading"
flourished for tens of thousands of years in the cognitive
dynamics of tracking among hunting and gathering cultures right back to paleolithic times. For whether ancient or
modern, the one thing good hunters know when they see
the tracks of an animal is that the animal isn't there. That's
all they know. And they know that's all they know as they
make meaning out of meaningless signs. Reading, pure and
simple. And storytelling, as they imagine where that animal
might have gone.

Humans have known this contradiction for a very long
time. To go back 40,000 years, people then were "reading"
images on walls like those discovered in the Chauvet caves.
They understood that those exquisitely painted horses were
horses. And that they weren't horses. I could have used their

wisdom when I encountered C-A-T in grade one. But we all have to learn this for ourselves.

* * *

There are many other competitive elements in storytelling in addition to those between performance and print, or words and images. Competition is often involved, as we have seen, in a struggle to affirm human agency and individual dignity over the indifference of the world out there. That is what Louis Riel was doing when he gave precedence and power to prayer over the military music being played by the North-West Mounted Police outside his prison cell window.

In a book called *The Educated Imagination*, which was taken from his 1962 Massey Lectures, the literary critic Northrop Frye wrote about how we give reality a human form—he called it making the environment into a home, a world we build for ourselves out of what we see. He could have called it the storytelling imagination, because what he was referring to was a world shaped by words—the words of stories and songs. It wasn't by chance that one of his last books, on the Bible, was called *Words with Power*. Making the environment into a home was for him a deeply human enterprise—a form of resistance to those pressures of reality that Wordsworth and Thoreau warned against and that storytellers going back millennia have defied with their words. In Frye's opinion it was a balance between defiance and dedication when it came to reality, as well as a competition between the human and the natural world—the imagination transforming the place where we find ourselves into the place where we want to live. We begin with a cultural storyline, and then with names and new knowledge and craft and construction in an enterprise both heroic and hazardous, and one that seems deeply human. Heroic for us, and all too often hazardous to the environment as we make it over based on a storyline that we inherit from our language and culture, building shelters and gathering places and recreational spaces inspired by our existing storytelling narratives and ignoring the ways in which new relationships with the environment, and new storylines, can benefit both our material and our spiritual lives. Then whatever we come up with, we organize entire societies according to this storytelling, and we confirm the storyline in the covenants and constitution we create. But inertia is a majestic force in both storytelling and the way of life it sustains, and it sometimes lets us forget that if we want to change our world, we can—and must—change our stories. That is the kind of change that challenges us right now.

For the story we choose to base our constructs on is one that shapes—and sometimes mis-shapes—the world to make ourselves comfortable, and to ensure our survival. One such story, immensely popular for over 300 years, is told in Daniel Defoe's novel *Robinson Crusoe*, which put humans in the spell of wants and needs, shaped by storytelling, to find a home in the "wilderness"—itself a made-up category full of the contradictions and uncertainty of storytelling itself. Some origin stories put humans in competition and often in conflict with each other, but almost always they involve our relationship with the natural world—a world whose majestic indifference to us suggests that we may always be strangers, outcasts and castaways in it. And so we do what we do best: we make up stories about this. Whence many of the world's myths.

Like many good stories, *The Life and Strange, Surprising Adventures of Robinson Crusoe* has a basis in reality, not just the broadly human reality I have described but a specific human experience. Alexander Selkirk was a sailor who was marooned on an island off the coast of Chile in 1704. Selkirk told the story of his time there to Woodes Rogers, the ship captain who found and rescued him. Rogers then retold Selkirk's story in a book about his travels across the oceans of the world, and soon Selkirk's story was widely known and caught the attention of a journalist named Daniel Defoe, who turned it into *Robinson Crusoe*.

But Selkirk's story doesn't end there, and there is a connection between it and one of the great survival anthems of our age. An eighteenth-century English poet named William Cowper also took up Selkirk's story and wrote a popular poem titled "Verses supposed to be written by Alexander Selkirk." "I am monarch of all I survey," it begins, "My right there is none to dispute; / From the centre all round to the sea, / I am lord of the fowl and the brute." I'm not very fond of those lines, but Cowper's poem got a fair bit of attention, and he was well known, with no less a literary contemporary than Samuel Taylor Coleridge calling him England's best modern poet. Cowper himself would soon become a household name, not because of this poem but because of his collaboration with one Reverend John Newton in writing a series of several hundred hymns to go along with weekly sermons in the little village of Olney in England where they lived. One of these was Cowper's celebrated hymn "God moves in a mysterious way, / His wonders to perform." Another, by Newton, a former slave-ship captain turned abolitionist, was "Amazing Grace," a hymn that eventually set the all-time record for crossover hits, and for chanting down the Babylons of personal as well as public crises. You never can tell when stories and songs will find us, and where they will take us.

★ ★ ★

"I once was lost and now I'm found." Lost and found has been a powerful storyline for a very long time, and it has an influence on almost all self-help storytelling. One form this takes is in the competition—often internalized but no less real—between success and failure, a competition that storytelling has been taking as its subject for a long time, often turning it around so that what seems like failure is redeemed as success.

Failure as success is the story, described in the previous chapter, of the sacredness of suffering. It is there, as we saw, at the centre of the Christian story and of the great annual Sun Dance of the Indigenous peoples of the Plains. It is there in the Bhagavad Gita, the song of God at the heart of Hinduism. And it has long appealed both to storytellers and to all those who have difficulty determining how to keep winning and losing in balance—which is all of us, at least some of the time.

Science and religion, in different ways, are also located within storytelling traditions of lost and found. Both describe navigating from being lost (the "what is this all about" state of mind) to being found (with its cries of "Eureka" for science and "Hallelujah" for religion).

★ ★ ★

Often it is our greatest storytellers who give us that promise of balance that Joy Harjo described—a promise that, like balance itself, is always precarious. This precarious balance is certainly evident in the origin stories of many of the world's settler societies. But it is sometimes lost in our determination to celebrate settlers as winners in the struggle for survival. When I think of such storylines, I immediately call to mind our national anthems. I am also reminded of a passage at the end of James Joyce's novel *A Portrait of the Artist as a Young Man* in which his hero, Stephen Dedalus, announces that he is going "to forge in the smithy of [his] soul the uncreated conscience of [his] race." The word *forge* is carefully chosen to catch the contradiction: it's both a forging and a forgery.

One settler story that fits this description begins with the simple phrase "Columbus discovered America." It is almost laughable in its untruth, and in its influence almost unimaginable. Although the phrase wasn't coined in 1492, its imperial power was felt immediately, for Columbus's "discovery" was followed *just one year later* by the so-called Doctrine of Discovery. It came not from an enterprising Spanish pen but from the Catholic Pope. And it sanctioned, indeed encouraged, the taking—the theft—of Indigenous homelands by European imperial powers without any negotiation with their inhabitants under the breathtaking and brutal legal logic that such lands were *terra nullius*, land belonging to no one. Nobody's land.

That word *nobody* was a storyteller's trick, of course. But it had consequences that have a grim echo in a popular little poem written in 1899 by American writer Hughes Mearns:

> Yesterday, upon the stair,
> I met a man who wasn't there
> He wasn't there again today
> I wish, I wish he'd go away.

It is the last line that always haunts me, for the story of settler/Indigenous relations for the past 500 years has been a story of wishing and wishing those nobodies who weren't there would go away. And planning ways to make that happen. The best way was that first way, the wretched designation of "undeveloped" Indigenous homelands as empty. And its Indigenous inhabitants as nobodies. Not even persons. Just "inconvenient Indians," to use writer Thomas King's memorable coinage.

Let's go back to the beginning. Not the beginning of Indigenous civilizations—that would take us back at least 15,000 years here in North America, and 50,000 years if we were in Asia or Africa or Australia—but the beginning of contacts between settlers and Indigenous societies in the Americas. We know that contact began at least several centuries before Christopher Columbus, with travel by Norse and possibly African sailors to the islands and mainland along the east coast of the Americas, and travellers from

Asia and the Pacific Islands arriving on the west coast. But Columbus and his 1492 arrival get most of the attention, and I think it is fair to say that the settlement it sponsored has caused much of the trouble. Columbus discovered America, we are sometimes *still* told. Good on him, some might say, for he was a brave navigator and opened one of the world's great migration routes. But "Columbus discovered America" is a brutally stupid sentence—one that became a sentence of exile for Indigenous people, its "new world" fantasy devastating their homelands and obliterating their very-old-world heritage. And despite its transparent nonsense, even now this statement is as traumatic for many Indigenous people as Holocaust denial is for Jewish people, for it denies their humanity. And as with Jewish people, the past is present for most Indigenous peoples across Canada and around the world. And for them the personal is certainly political.

Of course, Columbus didn't know where he was, so he couldn't know what he had "discovered." But since he had been seeking a passage to India, he let his imagination take over and called the first people he met Indians. The imagination is a powerful instrument, and people quickly picked up on this story and his supposed discovery. It was what we would now call fake news, for of course this so-called world and its citizens weren't new at all.

A few of the early arrivals recognized this, especially one whose name, Bartolomé de las Casas, should be better known. And so should his story. Las Casas arrived as a layman ten years after Columbus, became a Dominican priest, and in that role took the lead in arguing against what was already, within a decade of Columbus's arrival, an institutionalized definition and oppression of Indigenous people as nobodies. He insisted on their treatment not as primitive savages, as they were seen by most newcomers, but as rational and civilized people who were sustained by a strict set of customs, laws, spiritual beliefs and time-tested harvesting practices. He proposed that relationships with them should be governed by the authority of *their* systems as much as by those of the European newcomers. And he declared this not only to his fellow travellers to the Caribbean but to a wide audience back in his native Spain. People heard him, but for the next 500 years far too few listened.

For truth be told, most of his fellow travellers had their eyes peeled for nobodies, savage nobodies. However, since few of the people they encountered behaved savagely to the newcomers—quite the contrary—let's take up another term they used: *Barbarians*. The word itself tells the story. It comes to English from a word the Greeks coined to describe the Persians, who didn't speak Greek and whose language sounded to the Greeks like "ba-ba-ba" nonsense. The Greeks knew that Persian civilization went back millennia— *but* they didn't speak Greek. And they behaved differently from the Greeks. That was all that was needed to identify them as barbarians. For the early settlers in the Americas, anyone who didn't speak one of the "civilized" European languages was childlike. Possibly savage. Certainly primitive. And there was another string to this imperial storytelling bow that had to do with their "primitive" behaviour. They wandered over the land, the story went. Civilized people, like the newcomers, settled down and developed it. It was only right for the newcomers to get on with doing just that. The Pope said so.

The Doctrine of Discovery and the phrase "*terra nullius*" mask a fake story, a forgery that needs to be put into competition with the hundreds of true histories of heritage and homeland told by Indigenous peoples. I emphasize *histories* in the plural because some have a habit of calling for a single Indigenous history, *one* history that tells the truth. That's an imperial storytelling gambit in colonial dress—a cover for running roughshod over both the subtle and the substantial differences in how Indigenous peoples experienced first encounters and subsequent relationships with settler society, and the differences in storytelling ways that describe these experiences, ways that are shaped by particular Indigenous languages and ceremonial traditions and spiritual beliefs.

★ ★ ★

For all their sometimes admirable contributions to our lives, and to some recent decisions by our senior courts affirming Indigenous sovereignty and personhood, councils of church and state and law have for hundreds of years often acted as apologists for settler development at the expense of Indigenous land rights and national identity. In the years after Columbus, it was lawyers and jurists in Europe and then in the Americas who provided legitimacy to the European imperial domination of the newly "discovered" lands, joining not only avaricious commercial and political advocates but also philosophical and religious apologists for what we now call globalization. The time-honoured way of taking over land was by military force, but now it was by way of the more convenient and much more efficient force of religious edicts such as the Doctrine of Discovery and legal arguments such as those later outlined in 1758 by a Swiss jurist named Emmerich de Vattel in *The Law of Nations*, which codified the idea of *terra nullius*.

At the end of the day, however, it was all a cover for a 500-year war against the Indians, using force to implement and obscure the forgery. Over and over again, settler societies enacted legislation to enforce this newcomer family compact. Canada put in place the Indian Act in 1876, just after Confederation, formalizing a kind of wardship in which "primitive" Indigenous people would be deprived of much of their homeland, separated on reserves—essentially refugee camps for the homeless—and encouraged or forced to take up "civilized" habits and religious beliefs on the way to their eventual assimilation. The Gradual Civilization Act, passed a few years earlier, signalled the storyline.

The same pattern was happening all over the world. Australia's founding legislation, passed in 1901, proposed that "in reckoning the numbers of people of the Commonwealth, or of a State, or other part of the Commonwealth, Aboriginal natives shall not be counted." This section was not amended until 1967, and although it was surrounded by complicated legal fictions within which it had a kind of justification, in the final analysis it represented a simple belief: Aborigines are not to be counted because they do not count. They are nobodies.

When I was in Australia in the 1980s, the government of the time proposed a new Bill of Rights to acknowledge the presence of Aboriginal peoples in the country. I remember a cartoon that appeared in a local paper, with one Aboriginal Australian talking to another. "A bill of rights?" he said. "I thought we paid that one." This cartoon chimed nicely with the slogan of the Aboriginal sovereignty movement that had wide currency at the time. "Pay the Rent," it demanded of the government. Aboriginal Australians were responsible landlords, the campaign noted, with no wish to throw their tenants out. They knew all too well what that was like. But they wanted to negotiate the rent. Including the back rent. Several hundred years' worth.

★ ★ ★

To give a sense of how persistent the storyline I have just outlined has been over the past 500 years, here are a few lines from a morality play written in 1520, less than thirty years after Columbus's voyage, by John Rastell. He was a distinguished lawyer, a member of parliament in England, and he was married to the sister of the renowned Renaissance humanist Sir (now Saint) Thomas More. Like many Europeans at that time, he was fascinated by the stories that came back at almost internet speed from the early new world adventurers. But like most of them, it seems Rastell hadn't heard of Bartolomé de las Casas. And he wrote these lines:

> And what a great and meritorious dede
> It were to have the people instructed
> To lyve more Vertuously

And to lerne to know of man the maner
And also to knowe of god theyr maker
Which as yet lyve all bestly

Instructions on how to change from living "all beastly"
to living "more Vertuously"—how to change from savage to civilized, how to become a somebody rather than a
nobody—this from the heart of the humanities in the person of Thomas More's brother-in-law.

It might be grim comfort to us that those words come
from long ago and far away. But they don't, for the words
themselves and the ideas they represent are very much
still with us. As recently as 1991 the chief justice of the
British Columbia Supreme Court, and later chancellor
of the University of British Columbia, Allan McEachern,
dismissed the Aboriginal rights of two confederated First
Nations in the province—Gitxsan and Wet'suwet'en—by
discounting their ancestors as nobodies. Since they had
"no wheeled vehicles, no written literature," he wrote in his
decision, they were "unorganized societies"—that was his
legal phrase—"roaming from place to place like beasts of
the field." No writing. No civilization. No humanity. Living
all beastly, as John Rastell wrote 500 years ago.

Yet Judge McEachern's considered statement was written almost yesterday. And it came from an intelligent and
(in the opinion of people who knew him well) decent person
who had just spent 318 trial days hearing testimony from
expert settler society witnesses describing the sophisticated
and affluent lives of these hunting and gathering First
Nations communities over thousands of years, a history also

and more authoritatively presented in traditional stories and songs performed by distinguished Indigenous elders who had been schooled in them from childhood. Two of the most respected Gitxsan elders testified to the importance of the gift that salmon offer when they make themselves available to them as spiritual as well as material nourishment. But as he dismissed their testimony, the judge described them as just "two old men who like fishing." Of all the vicious things he said in his judgment, that was the one that hurt many Gitxsan the most.

Fortunately, Judge McEachern's crude and insulting decision was sternly rejected a few years later by the Supreme Court of Canada. In its decision, the court affirmed both the civilized history and the constitutional status of Indigenous peoples in Canada and directed trial judges in the future to accept the integrity and authority of Indigenous traditions of orality. This case was called *Delgamuukw*, after the elder in whose name it was originally put forward, and it has become the point of reference for acknowledgements of Indigenous sovereignty and land rights that are beginning to change the story of Canada and to establish a firm foundation for reconciliation.

Despite the progress, it is hard not to be worried that 500 years after Columbus, intelligent people were still talking about Indigenous people as "roaming from place to place like beasts of the field." Those who continue along this line are not necessarily stupid. But they are certainly ignorant. And stories are needed to enlighten them. When they are not dismissed as the ramblings of "two old men who like fishing," Indigenous histories of homeland and heritage are by far the best competition against ignorance of this kind, and against the Doctrine of Discovery (which, 500 years later, has not yet been withdrawn by the Catholic Church). Histories about the beginnings of Indigenous settlement in the Americas from different nations and confederacies need to be put forward in both print and performance to finish it off for good.

There is a phrase Jamaicans use for a story or a saying that should be forgotten: "It need fi dead." The Doctrine of Discovery "need fi dead." So do all those old imperial stories that have caused so much damage. And they need to be replaced not just with stories that chronicle the damage, important as these stories are, but also with storytelling that celebrates Indigenous *settlement* in their homelands and their remarkable survival in the face of the storytelling sponsored by the Doctrine of Discovery. These histories also take us much further back, telling about territorial stewardship and affluent living as well as climate changes and environmental disasters and social upheavals far more drastic than the ones we face right now, but which their people adapted to and lived through. Their science and spirituality, which has helped them survive, will help us, if they are willing to share it. Few would blame them if they were not ready to do so yet.

One such Indigenous story from those early times was told by my late friend Neil Sterritt, who led his people to trial in the *Delgamuukw* case and later wrote a remarkable book titled *Mapping My Way Home: A Gitxsan History*. It brings the mysterious crafts of wayfinding, the enigmatic truths of history, and the dreamlike realities of home together in one remarkable adventure and survival story, covering tens of thousands of years of Indigenous human enterprise and experience until his people eventually settled in what became their homeland—the mountains of northwest British Columbia along the Skeena, "the river of mists." Neil reminds us that to these first peoples of the Americas, "for at least 14,000 years, the rest of the world did not exist."

Like the famous cartographer Mercator, Sterritt offers us a new way of mapping and navigating the world, not by imagining curved surfaces as straight lines, as Mercator did, but by taking the two classic metaphors of genealogy—the tree and the river—and combining them with the two models of history that geology proposes: time as an arrow and time as a cycle. He does this with a storyteller's instinct for unlikely moments, unforgettable people and unmistakable words and deeds. And with a bit of mischief.

His story begins with that defining moment when humans make a new place their home, naming the rivers and mountains and plants and animals, building settlements and harvesting resources and creating secular and sacred customs that reflect their imaginations and desires as well as their realities and needs. For all of us in the Americas, this is the moment when the first peoples—*Alungigat*, in the Gitxsan language—settled throughout the northern and southern Americas, the moment when the first wanderers became the first settlers. Later along came some newcomers whom the Gitxsan called *K'amksi'waa*. It is their word for driftwood, bleached white and coming and going with the flow of the river and the tide of the sea in a new wave of wandering.

This is the history that Neil Sterritt offers us. And it is an inspiring one, reversing the settler/wanderer story that has plagued relations between Indigenous and non-Indigenous peoples around the world for centuries, and giving agency to his people by rendering a Gitxsan history that celebrates what he calls a confluence of fresh water and salt water, river and sea, *Alungigat* and *K'amksi'waa*. For in this wayfinder's mapping, the first peoples are the settlers of this land, and the newcomers are the wanderers, the nomads. But they too, the people of my heritage, want to make a home in this new world. His book gives us a lesson in how that has been done in Gitxsan territory, and how it has sometimes been undone; and it reminds us that doing so with respect is a work in progress.

★ ★ ★

There's a song by Bob Marley called "Duppy Conqueror." It is about breaking free from the power of a duppy, a ghost or spirit of the dead whose burial rites have been incomplete. The spirit wanders homeless, ready to be captured by others with evil on their minds. Then, instead of being an ancestral protector, the duppy becomes an evil presence.

"Let us bury our dead" was a cry I heard often in Aboriginal Australia. Just now I mentioned my time in Australia when the phrase "Pay the Rent" was taken up by advocates of Indigenous sovereignty. On one occasion, I visited an Aboriginal camp just north of Alice Springs, where I spent time with a group of Aboriginal men and women from across Australia who had gathered to discuss what to do about their homelands, which were haunted by restless spirits who might someday become their duppies if they couldn't find a way to pay their respects and complete the spiritual cycle of the ancestors in a good way. They talked about many things, but in the evening, after a day of dealing with details, they talked about those ancestors, some of whose bodies and spirits were resting uneasily as museum exhibits or skeleton curiosities, appropriated as someone else's heritage, part of an imperialism that turned ancestors into artifacts, and atrocities into anecdotes. Many had died alone and unremembered, waiting for proper burial. Other ancestors of these men and women had been lost from sight. The land where their spirits remained had fallen into other hands, and the spirits wandered homeless. So, in a sense, did many of their descendants, those with whom I was sharing a meal around cooking fires set in old oil drums, and talking under a clear, cold desert sky. These men and women did not want to be duppy "conquerors." They wanted to bury their dead in a respectful way. And so I often put the phrase "Bury the Dead" together with "Pay the Rent" to remind myself of the spiritual as well as the material elements of life that have to come together if truth and reconciliation are to mean anything at all. And if our country is to be made whole.

There is a story I tell with residential schools much on my mind. At the end of Homer's epic *Iliad*, the triumphant Greek warrior Achilles drags the body of the fallen Trojan leader Hector in the dust around the walls of the city until finally, on the command of the ruler and protector god Zeus, he delivers up the body for a proper burial. "Thus held they funeral for Hector, tamer of horses." These are the last lines of the epic, one of the greatest in settler history, and the return to a sense of ceremony is as powerful as anything in that story of love and war. It keeps the terror of the unburied, unrespected dead at a distance, paradoxically by bringing the atrocity close to us. And those last words are not only the celebration of a hero, his people's only hope. They also are a tribute to an ordinary man. A tamer of horses. The Homeric version of an auto mechanic. All of a sudden, in those final words, workers as well as warriors become important. And spiritual as well as material values come into a new kind of balance—a storytelling kind that can redeem our world. In a poem titled "Fates Worse Than Death," the Canadian poet Don McKay tells the story. "Atrocity," he begins,

> implies an audience of gods.
> The gods watched as swiftfooted
> godlike Achilles cut behind the tendons of
>   both feet
> and pulled a strap of oxhide through
> so he could drag the body of Hektor,
> tamer of horses, head down in the dust
> behind his chariot.
> Some were appalled, some not,
> having nursed their grudges well, until
> those grudges were fine milkfed
> adolescents, armed
> with automatic weapons. The gods,
> and farther off,

the gods before the gods, those who ate
their children and contrived
exquisite tortures in eternity, watched
and knew themselves undead. Such is the loss,
   such
the wrath of swiftfooted godlike
Achilles, the dumb fucker, that he drags,
up and down, and round and round the tomb
of his beloved, the body of Hektor,
tamer of horses. Atrocity
is never senseless. No. Atrocity is dead ones
locked in sense, forbidden
to return to dust, but scribbled in it

★ ★ ★

Sometimes—indeed in science, quite often—a storyline changes suddenly with those "Eureka" or "Hallelujah" moments introducing stories that defy easy understandings but illuminate new possibilities. Just as in the story I am going to tell, when a few words overturned authoritarian "overstandings." A Jamaican friend of mine, Barry Chevannes, was one of the leading scholars of Rastafari. He was not a Rasta himself but was very widely respected in the close-knit Rastafarian communities across the island, some of whom used to refer to him as the "plainclothes Rasta." During a progressive period in Jamaica politics in 2000, he was appointed chair of a National Commission on Ganja to recommend steps the government might take towards decriminalizing or possibly legalizing marijuana, the use of which was criminalizing far too many young people and, along the way, damaging far too many lives. But also central to the issue, and one reason for its urgency, was the use of ganja in Rastafarian religious observance, the equivalent of incense in many Christian denominations and sweetgrass and sage in Indigenous ceremonial traditions.

Barry agreed to the request to chair the committee, knowing that the government would also appoint several much less sympathetic citizens. But with his new colleagues and their various opinions he set about scheduling reviews of medical and legal research on the subject, as well as engaging in discussions with government authorities and knowledgeable citizens across the Americas and around the world, and holding extensive hearings across Jamaica, in which many Rastafarian leaders and devout brethren and sistren participated.

Barry told me that some members of the committee had seldom listened to any Rastafarians (even as they worried about their children joining them) despite the fact that Rastas were everywhere in the communities of Jamaica. But slowly his colleagues came to appreciate both the world wisdom and the spiritual dedication that Rastafari represented. Eventually, the mood of the committee shifted towards some sympathy with the idea of loosening the prohibitions against ganja use.

But the breakthrough still came as a complete surprise to everyone. It was on the occasion of an appearance by a distinguished Rasta elder and theologian from Montego Bay at one of the hearings. He came into the hearings room, said Barry, with the confidence of a spiritual truthteller. In the voice of an Old Testament prophet, he announced to the committee "Your work is done." Rastafarians themselves had discovered the answer, he said. Where? In the Bible, of course. During a reasoning session recently, one of the brethren had come up with a true interpretation of scripture that made the case clear for the decriminalization of ganja and its Rastafarian sacramental use. "Moses did not see God *in* the burning bush," said the elder from Montego Bay. "He saw God *by burning* the bush."

Barry said several on the committee raised their hands in ceremonial delight. Eureka and Hallelujah. This *was* a better story. And in short order they had unanimously agreed to recommend to the government "the decriminalisation of ganja for personal, private use by adults and for use as a sacrament for religious purposes." Sadly, the government changed soon after, but the Babylonian spell was broken.

There's nothing like a good surprise to make us believe, especially the surprise of what the poet Coleridge called the "dear gorgeous nonsense" of philosophy. He was referring to Plato at the time, not my Rasta friend Mortimo Planno or the elder from Montego Bay. But they were all wise philosophers. And good storytellers.

★ ★ ★

The British economist Barbara Ward used to speak of "planetary housekeeping," by which she meant supporting those in need both here and away and sustaining the environment with attention to its requirements and with care not to pollute it by action or inaction. The Viennese call a person who looks after a house for someone else a *hausbesorger*, a "house-worrier." Accepting that kind of worry about the wider world of humanity as well as the environments in which we live can be invigorating, especially when it is inspired by storytelling that tells us what happened in places where we think nothing much ever happened. Often those things are happening right now, and in places close at hand, and those stories can help us all be good housekeepers. And since we can never be sure which stories or songs will do this best, we need to be open to many kinds—to everyday stories and music as well as those from other places and times.

Sometimes we find these stories and hear that music in the actions and ideas of good people, and in the stories they tell. They are everywhere if we would just notice them. And if we don't recognize them or hear them around us right now, we can turn to storytelling to take us back in time and to another place to find such people and to find out what they did then that might inspire us now.

If we are hoping to find how others managed one of the most important and difficult balances, that between work and play, there is one storyteller, scientist and statesman from the nineteenth century who brought work and play out of competition and into a new kind of balance. His name was John Lubbock, and he did more than almost anyone else, in a step-by-step and often surprisingly straightforward way, to attend to "housekeeping" at home in the time and the place he lived. And since he was a gifted storyteller, he was also able to change house and home and work and play for the better for everyone. He is not as well known these days as some of his contemporaries, mostly I think because he did not have the ironic sensibility that appealed to many chroniclers of his English Victorian times. But in his day he was much admired.

Lubbock understood the need for some serious house-worrying, though he didn't need it for himself. Born Sir John Lubbock, he was relatively comfortable. But he recognized that many of the people he met every day, and often took for granted, were not. Life was anything but easy for them, and there seemed to be little prospect of any improvement. He was determined to do something about it.

When John Lubbock is remembered, it is often for his promotion of reading and listening to stories—a deceptively modest proposal that I'll get to in a moment. But what for me is most inspiring is that he recognized the needs that *preceded* storytelling—not only the need for books to be available to everyone, but for everyone to have the place and the time to read them and to talk about them, and then the opportunity to tell stories and sing songs themselves and to listen to others. The problem was that there was hardly any such leisure time for people working on the streets and in the shops of the cities and towns he knew well—the kind of people Charles Dickens wrote about, for whom eighty or ninety hours a week, often on their feet all day, was a standard work schedule. And even if they had the time, there were few places such as public parks where they could gather and play games and have picnics and tell stories, and very few lending libraries where they could get books to read. Many weren't desperately impoverished even though they were poor, but they were physically, morally and spiritually exhausted. Of course, things were not easy in the countryside either. But Lubbock, who saw the working poor every day in his city of London, wanted to help his people.

So he got himself elected to parliament and immediately put forward legislation—he called it the Early Closing Bill—to reduce the civilized brutality of the long workdays for retail workers. It infuriated many of the store owners, but it relieved and refreshed their workers. Then he put forward another bill to establish the first annual holiday since the seventeenth-century Puritan purge of all holidays except Christmas and Good Friday. Until Lubbock took the lead, nobody had given any thought or taken any steps to replace even one of the many holy days that had been enjoyed in medieval times. He named this new holiday a Bank Holiday, a dull enough name designed to escape parliamentary scrutiny from the fat cats who wanted industry and thrift rather than complaints from the poor. And it passed with readings in the House of Commons that Lubbock arranged to take place late in the evening when most politicians likely to oppose it had gone home to enjoy their privileged leisure. The Bank Holiday became the first secular holiday in the history of Great Britain.

The name might have been modest, but its popularity was overwhelming. And so in short order was the author's, for the holiday was almost immediately called Saint Lubbock's Day by a grateful public. At first, there was only one Bank Holiday, set on the first Monday in August when the weather was likely to be at its best, but soon there were four each year.

Never one to rest easy, Lubbock then promoted legislation to expand public parks, where games could be played and picnics enjoyed, and to establish lending libraries in both the cities and the towns so that working men and women could take out books and read them. And it was books that gave his name new storytelling renown. He collaborated with the publisher George Routledge to publish a series of what became known as Sir John Lubbock's Hundred Books, available in sturdy but inexpensive bindings. Not necessarily the *best* books, he insisted, but simply *good* books, chosen with the help of friends and many in translation from all over the world. He was a devout churchgoer, but he had unqualified admiration for many non-Christian texts as long as they told entertaining stories, and he included the Qur'an and a book about Buddha along with the Bible, as well as the works of Confucius. Also included were an anthology of the poetry of China, poetic storytelling from south and central Asia and North Africa, philosophical and political meditations from the Middle East as well as northern and southern Europe, and some new books about science (though he said that science was changing so fast in all fields that it was hard to select ones that would last).

Together, these were books that he hoped would give pleasure, which was always his first principle in storytelling. And one of his favourite sayings, which has become one of mine, was a phrase he found in the writings of Richard de Bury, a bishop of Durham in the fourteenth century when books were just becoming available. Celebrating the fact that stories were now available in print, he said, "If you are ignorant, they [books] cannot laugh at you." To which Lubbock added, "The feeling that books are real friends is constantly present to all who love reading."

Lubbock's thoughts about the ephemeral nature of contemporary scientific inquiry was not an amateur speculation, for he was also a very important scientist. He had begun his serious scientific work with what he called pre-historic archaeology, a field of study that he effectively established as a scientific discipline, and for which he coined the terms *paleolithic* and *neolithic* to describe early phases of human work and play. Then he took up one of his early enthusiasms and became a distinguished naturalist, cited by Darwin in his *Origin of Species*. And he matched his geographical, botanical and environmental research with his own easy-to-read storytelling style, becoming very widely known for his lively discussion and debate about the natural as well as the human history of the world.

But *knowing* things was only part of the story for him, and this is where his light shines especially brightly for us. Not knowing and wondering about things were where science began for him, and he was always comfortable with the unknown and pleased to find stories about what we don't know or don't understand, believing that "what we know is an absolutely infinitesimal fraction of what we do not know. There is no single substance in Nature the uses and properties of which are yet completely known to us," he said. "There is no animal or plant the whole life-history of which we have yet unraveled. We are surrounded by forces and influences of which we understand nothing, and which we are as yet but dimly commencing to perceive. We live in a world of mystery, which we darken rather than explain by the use of terms which can neither define nor explain."

Lubbock was determined to keep wonder and wondering alive. "Many savage nations worship trees," he wrote, using language that makes us uncomfortable. But then he continues in a manner that we can only admire: "And I really think my first feeling would be one of delight and interest rather than surprise, if some day when I am alone in a wood one of the trees were to speak to me."

John Lubbock was not a simple man. But he believed in storytelling. And he believed in people, maintaining a wonderful counterculture instinct throughout his life, nourished by a scientist's healthy worry about maybe, just maybe, being wrong about things. And although he lived and worked within them, he was almost uniquely independent of institutional categories, and his remarkable achievements were nourished by a curiosity that was never far from childlike. With a youngster's appetite, he listened to people and told their stories, many of which were very moving. Speaking at the fiftieth jubilee of the Manchester Public Library in 1903, he told of "a Manchester woman who was taken on a trip to the seaside, which she had never visited. When she saw the sea, she was delighted. She said it was the first time in her life she had ever seen anything of which there was enough for everybody." I defy anyone hearing a comment like that to walk away unaffected. Lubbock knew about and listened to the people of his time.

Finally, he loved setting stories in genial and spirited competition with each other. Late in his life, he was made Lord Avebury in recognition of his work to preserve the ancient stone circles in England (especially those at Avebury near Stonehenge). And even, or especially, in that dignified role he liked telling stories against himself, stories in which he looked like a sophisticated fool in the presence of straightforward common sense. One story particularly delighted him.

"Do you know how these stones were made?" he asked a countryman standing next to a pile of stones in a Norwich field, where much earlier Lubbock had discovered the first fossil of a musk-ox that both their ancestors had probably hunted.

"Why, sir, I 'spect they growed, same as 'taturs," answered the man.

"Well," rejoined Lubbock, a lifetime of association with the greatest geologists and naturalists at the ready, "but if they lay there for fifty years, they would not get any bigger."

"No, sir, of course they wouldn't. Same as 'taturs. Take 'taturs out of the ground and they stops growin'."

A simple soul and a sophisticated scientist, we might say, shaking our head sadly. "No," Lubbock would happily answer, "two scientists walking along different storylines."

CHAPTER SIX

Truth and Belief

There's an old riddle about the mythical Greek philosopher-poet Epimenides, who said "Cretans are always liars."

Epimenides was himself from Crete. Was he telling the truth? Yes and no.

If he was telling the truth—that is, if Cretans are always liars—then he is lying.

And if he is lying when he says that Cretans are always liars, then since he just lied, he must be telling the truth.

IN THIS REALM OF CIRCULAR STORYTELLING, NO MATTER HOW much we crave certainty, we have to settle for uncertainty, and no matter how much we crave truth, we have to settle for belief—and to find some pleasure, some order, in a balance between them. Bewilderment has never hindered us, as we know from the truth of a round earth and the belief that we are sitting or standing right side up right now. Truth may triumph. But belief rules.

From our beginnings in the mountains or on the desert or by the seashore, belief has been central to the survival of humanity, whether it is belief in those early drawings and carvings and momentary gods, or whether it is those images and words from whose meaningless signs and sounds we created a storytelling world—a world where things happen that don't and C-A-TS are cats and not cats. But it was also in those beginnings that we learned to believe and not believe at the same time, to become comfortable with yes and no, with wonder and with wondering. Which is to say, with the idea of truth.

I say the idea of truth, because as we have seen truth is not as absolute as we might like to . . . to what? To believe? Truth and belief are close kin, and their relationships are not always friendly. But they are bound together by family ceremonies. Both are necessary. Neither is enough on its own. A promise of balance is what keeps them together and what sustains storytelling. Or as I have been suggesting in this book, maybe it's the other way around: storytelling keeps truth and belief together in the kind of teeter-totter balance that is life itself.

Left on their own, belief and truth become teenage rebels, demanding independence even as they depend upon support. Here is a story told by the American folklorist Barre Toelken about an Indigenous woman he invited from a northern California nation to come to the University of Oregon, where he was working at the time, to teach basket weaving. A large number of students, especially local crafts-people, enrolled in the four-week class, and at the end of the third week many of them, who had paid quite a bit to take the class and wanted to learn how to weave from somebody who knew the traditional way, were becoming quite frustrated because they hadn't yet done any basket weaving. All they had learned was some songs.

"We love these songs," they said, "but when do we get to the baskets?"

The Indigenous weaver looked confused and said, "That's what we're doing. A basket is a song made visible." A happening that was not happening—but which was, right then, in the songs they had been singing.

We believe her, and we want to believe her story. But the truth is we also want to make baskets. How do we bring this into balance? In one sense, her story does that, for whether we realize it or not, it offers the familiar comfort of storytelling, giving us a way of believing and not believing at the same time. After all, just as the basket weaver described a basket as a song made visible, we might think of a national anthem as a nation made audible. And although we pride ourselves on saying that the truth will save us, it is belief—belief in the contradictions and uncertainties of storytelling—that does so.

And for that balance I keep coming back to, truth always has a familiar house-worrier warning us about lies while belief has a cranky cousin we call doubt, which if left on its own generates all sorts of unease and fosters unbelief. But we like to believe. We want to believe. We need to believe. And so along comes storytelling, managing the unease that goes along with uncertainty and doubt by celebrating human truth—which we know is sometimes different from "absolute" truth, whatever that might be—in a storyline that we can surrender to. Such storytelling can help us find truth in a balance between belief and doubt.

Such truth is often bracketed together with beauty, as it was in a famous line by John Keats affirming that "beauty is truth, truth beauty—that is all ye know on earth, and all ye need to know." But a good poet is a storyteller, in this case inviting us to wonder what a subtle and subjective concept such as beauty is doing in the stern company of truth. Well, it turns out that they are close cousins, for ideals of beauty are just as determined by culture and language and often by place and time as ideals of truth are decided by the different ways of thinking and feeling that language and culture and the environment generate. So neither beauty nor truth on their own can claim to be universal, but together they seem to offer the kind of balance that belief has with doubt. And no matter how relative to language and culture the ideals of truth and beauty may be, the idea that there are some things we identify as true and beautiful seems to be fairly widely accepted across cultures and languages.

The connection between them can still be as mysterious as a riddle, and although they may not seem to be both truth and beauty are at the center of the riddle I used as the epigraph to this chapter. Epimenides was a semi-mythical Cretan who supposedly lived in the sixth century BCE. His reputation has lived on and bewildered readers in story-tellings as different as the Bible and the mathematical writings of the twentieth-century philosopher Bertrand Russell. And the contradiction in his story has inspired and infuriated many people. But for those of us interested in stories and songs, it also highlights the uncertainty and the contradiction and competition that storytelling cherishes, matching its opening question "Was he telling the truth?" with that familiar flourish, yes and no. And the elusive style of a riddle like this reminds us that style can be another name for beauty. Mysterious and magical.

In stories, contradiction and competition are always on display, and style is often apparent. As Oscar Wilde said, "truth is entirely and absolutely a matter of style. It is style that makes us believe in a thing, nothing but style." He wrote this in an essay (widely read at the time) called "The Decay of Lying," in which he lamented what he felt was the sorry state of fiction in his time—reminding us that the Latin word *facere* (to make) is the root of both *fiction* and *fact*. All stories are made up, like tools and language, beauty and truth.

In a poem titled "The Idea of Order at Key West," the American poet Wallace Stevens listens to a woman singing a beautiful song about the sea and is filled with wonder at how she brings to life her subject and the scene. She was "the single artificer of the world in which she sang," he says, and credits her with the truth and beauty she creates in her storytelling song. But spellbound by the wonder of the moment, he is left with the other listeners on the shore wondering "Whose spirit is this? . . . because we knew it was the spirit that we sought and knew that we should ask this often as she sang." Whose spirit? That of the sea, the singer, or the song? The teller or the tale or its telling? Like the uncertainty all storytelling celebrates, it is the question rather than the answer that sustains our wonder, nourishes our wondering, and helps us survive.

Here are a few words from the humanist and scientist Jacob Bronowski describing how different kinds of story-telling can bring together not only reason and imagination but belief and truth: "Many people believe that reasoning, and therefore science, is a different activity from imagining," he writes,

> but this is a fallacy. The child that discovers that he [or she] can make images and move them around in their head has entered the same gateway to imagination and to reason. Reasoning is constructed with movable images just as certainly as poetry is. You may have been told, you may still have the feeling, that $e=mc^2$ is not an imaginative statement. If so, you are mistaken. The symbols in that master-equation of the twentieth century—e for energy, and m for mass, and c for the speed of light—are images for absent things or concepts, of exactly the same kind as the words 'tree' or 'love' in a poem. The poet John Keats was not writing anything which (for him at least) was fundamentally different from an equation when he wrote [in "Ode on a Grecian Urn]
>
> > Beauty is truth, truth beauty—that is all
> > Ye know on earth, and all ye need to know.
>
> There is no difference in the use of such words as "beauty" and "truth" in the poem, and such symbols as "energy" and "mass" in the equation.

For all their differences, science and the arts, as well as religion, share a belief in the family relationships of truth and beauty in storytelling. They also share a belief, as Keats put it in a passage just before these lines, that beauty and truth remain inseparable "in midst of other woe than ours, a friend." And a belief that the wonders and wonderings that storytelling generates can help us and sometimes heal us with a promise of the balance that will keep us going through another season of uncertainty, of believing and not believing in a world that seems indifferent to our hopes and dreams. That balance is the grace that Joy Harjo talked about, a balance that, in one form or another, we are all looking for—a balance that also offers a reconciliation of beauty and fear in a refreshingly new kind of truth. There is sometimes no balance better than a contradiction. It was and it was not. Believe it and not.

There's a long history of allegiance to beauty and its mysterious truth—and to truth and its mysterious beauty— in science. For some reason buried deep in the human heart and soul, we cannot seem to get away from this alliance. Earlier, I told how back in the sixth century BCE, the mathematician Pythagoras proposed that the earth was round because for him a sphere was the truest, most beautiful shape. Picking up on the beautiful precision of Einstein's famous equation, the twentieth-century American philosopher and educator Scott Buchanan said that "the best proofs in mathematics are short and crisp like epigrams and the longest have swings and rhythms that are like music . . . The solemn sound of demonstrated mathematical proof is a professional [storyteller's] way of announcing an arrival at some point on a journey fantastic"—waving happily to those whose storytelling proofs it rivals and replaces, boasting "this is a better one." For boasting and toasting are as central to storytelling as truth-telling. Eureka and Hallelujah.

★ ★ ★

As I described in Chapter Two, the truth of—and the belief in—everything depends on a sense of ceremony. But also, and more than we sometimes realize, it may depend on *where* that ceremony takes place. Consider the statement "The sun rises in the east and sets in the west." That's about as simple as it gets. Absolutely, objectively, *universally* true, confirmed by everyone every day. Except, of course, that we know it's also absolutely, objectively, universally false. But it fits the facts of our everyday experience—our touchstone ceremony for many things—and anyway, by now it's just a figure of speech that we know not to take literally.

But there is something else, another ceremonial bias. If we were to try out that universal truth about the sun rising in the east and setting in the west on an Inuk or Inuvialuit or Yup'ik citizen in the north, or indeed anyone living above the Arctic Circle, they would say, "That's a lie." Their knowledge of the sun is unequivocally different. During midwinter, the sun surfaces slowly in the south at midday, stays for an hour or two, and then goes back under at nearly the same spot. In midsummer, the sun circles the sky, never setting. We therefore need to be a bit more cautious about our universal truths, even the ones, like the sunrise and sunset, that (if the world really *is* round) aren't true anyway. It's enough to make our head spin. Just like the round earth.

★ ★ ★

All storytelling ceremonies that claim to offer *the* truth are defined by protocols, often very strict ones. Few can match those that safeguard the laws of a community, perhaps because those laws are both particularly vulnerable and particularly precious. But as we have seen, even as they decide the truth according to the law our courts seem astonishingly ambivalent about whether they believe the teller or the tale.

One storytelling arena in which truth has a special premium and whose protocols are also surprisingly stern is education. As I mentioned earlier, it is one of our most common storytelling sites, with quite strict storytelling ceremonies in which we teachers tell truths—truths as *we* understand them, of course. We also show our students how to understand these truths, and believe them, while maintaining that balance between belief and doubt that we hope is almost automatic because we presume that they have all had a long association with storytelling. But at the end of the day or the year, we want our students to be able to say, relatively comfortably, that they remember and believe the truths we have told them and the beauties we have admired when they face their institutional judges and juries in the form of examinations and interviews. And if they pass muster, we give them "credit"—which is our way of saying "we believe that you believe what we believe to be true." And belief and truth dance off the convocation stage together.

But both belief and truth have a defiant streak, just as many students do. And I hope we always try to celebrate when their wonder turns into wondering and they realize that the uncertainties they know to be at the centre of all storytelling are there, too, at the centre of their educational curriculum—and recognize that, along with belief, doubt has always been central to survival.

★ ★ ★

There are almost as many challenges when it comes to the stories of science as there are with those of religion, and many of them involve language. Both scientific and religious stories are almost always in some form of translation—in science, translation from mathematical and technological and other realms of scientific inquiry, and in religion, often from ancient languages as incomprehensible as complex mathematics to many believers, and sometimes in messages from other-than-human sources. But the storytellers of science and religion both recognize the challenges and mask the awkwardness of the translation. And much of their storytelling is so good that we believe the truth of their stories. Of course, we may wonder what exactly it is that they are talking about—for example when they describe something being in two places at once or being both mortal and immortal—but that is part of their mysterious appeal, just as it is part of much good storytelling.

We frequently try to determine boundaries that separate the stories of science from those of religion—affording each its own authority without discrediting the other. After all, each is simply trying to make sense of the world, and the place of human life in it. And they each remind us, albeit in different ways, that some things don't make sense, and that there are some things we can't control. The difference is that the stories of religion show us how to accept these things. The stories of science show us that we don't always have to. "We're not sure" is the signature of good science, even as "we are sure" is the signature of its storytelling.

But like all good storytellers, those who speak in the arena of science *or* religion often intensify some of the mystery even as they clarify some of the meanings. The British biologist J.B.S. Haldane, writing in the 1920s, made a distinction that is useful in bringing together our attitudes towards them both, suggesting that

> religion is a way of life and an attitude to the
> universe. It brings us into closer touch with the
> inner nature of reality. Statements of fact made
> in its name are untrue in detail, but often
> contain truth at their core. Science is also a
> way of life and an attitude to the universe. It
> is concerned with everything but the nature of
> reality. Statements of fact made in its name are
> generally right in detail, but can only reveal the
> form, and not the real nature of existence.

Beyond these tidy categories, we need to remember that the wonder that beauty and truth create comes in various guises and does not always fall neatly into scientific or religious or artistic arrangements. Just ask the young people who routinely use the word *awesome* with wonderful disregard for any fussy concern about the hierarchy of occasions that merit it.

Wonder, pure wonder, is all that is required for belief. And it is often associated with new scientific truths. Hallelujah and Eureka are closer than we realize. For what science and religion have in common is that invitation to wonder.

There are also some fundamental questions about truth in the natural, physical and social sciences and in religion that have to do with relationships between the human and the non-human, as well as between the organic and the mechanical. Some of the most interesting recent models in contemporary science move across these boundaries in a way that takes Isaiah's prophecy—that "sooner or later every valley shall be exalted, and every mountain and hill shall be made low, and the crooked shall be made straight"—one step further into the different truth-telling of myth. I think of Canadian geophysicist Tuzo Wilson's theory of continental drift and plate tectonics, which changed our scientific understanding of the land we live on in a way that rhymed both with the ancient myth of the earth as the goddess Gaia and a much more modern myth (and an ancient one in some Indigenous storytelling) of the earth as a living organism. We need to get as good at making connections as we are at illuminating contradictions, opening up conversations between the truths and beliefs of different storytelling traditions to give ourselves a better perspective on their interdependence.

★ ★ ★

Tuzo Wilson's insight was a counterpart to the new knowledge of genetics that transformed natural history, and it put the deep time of geology into conversation with the disruptive and productive mutations of evolutionary theory. Knowing that the drifting and shifting he described would be hard for his colleagues to imagine, he came up with a paper model—like origami, the classic folding craft—to demonstrate how the enormous mobile plates of his tectonic theory are connected by ridges and trenches and fault lines. When he saw puzzled faces he would pull out his parlour trick and perform a storytelling modelling of the mystery of these earth movements. Storytelling as play, as well as work, bringing pleasure into the company of purposeful enterprise.

I have spoken a few times about the importance of play along with work, about the singer and the storyteller alongside the hunter and the *hausbesorger*, and about John Lubbock's lifetime of work on behalf of play. We have plenty of stories, though never enough, about working people in the world, and I certainly won't offer a catalogue. But the stories in this section provide a new perspective on a different kind of work—a kind that tends to get forgotten in our agricultural and industrial societies, but which catches the spirit of much of the work in the world.

One of these stories is from a traditional Innu caribou hunter in what is now Labrador. It is about the bringing together of choice and chance in a way comparable to the combination of diligent determination and good fortune that sustains scholarship and research in the conventional arts and sciences. The other, also from the north, turns to the storytelling of things made by human craft, often with exquisite care, to help people do the everyday things necessary to support and sustain a community. These things don't talk. But they tell a good story. And all good stories bring truth and beauty together and require belief in their storytelling if we are to appreciate them.

In a book titled *Caribou Hunter: A Song of a Vanished Innu Life* that I had the privilege of introducing a few years ago (in its English translation, from the original French by Serge Bouchard), an Innu caribou hunter from Labrador named Mathieu Mestokosho talked about what work meant to him. In his case, it was the hard work of hunting for survival. In speaking about it, he paid special tribute to elders of his tribe, technicians of sacred as well as secular well-being, who dreamed the hunt and did the things necessary to make it happen, praising their Creator and keeping their powder dry, merging theory and practice.

"To be successful using [the elders'] methods," says Mestokosho, "you had to *believe* in them." We have already seen how such belief is important in seafaring navigation; the conditions for success in hunting and fishing are much the same. On land and its rivers and lakes as well as at sea, uncertainty rules, repetition governs behaviour, and you wait for surprises. "You have to hunt constantly to have good luck," Mestokosho said, which means unceasing craft and care: making canoes and toboggans and snowshoes, making camp and breaking trail, stalking game and setting traps, baiting the grounds and building the flakes (platforms to clean, dry and salt fish), never wasting anything and always watching for trouble, planning ahead and learning from the past—all in order to be ready for those moments when the caribou or the cod offer themselves, or when the island you are seeking comes into sight and meaning becomes clear.

Then there are those seemingly ordinary things, the material objects of the working world that are important for their personal and practical connection, their careful craft, their beauty *and* their usefulness. Such everyday works of careful craft offer storytelling insight that few other forms of storytelling can match, showing how "everything that is made—all the implements and adornments of life—causes us to remember" the craft and the courage of people to whom we don't usually pay much attention. The phrase is Ann Fienup-Riordan's from a catalogue she wrote for an exhibition titled *Yuungnaqpiallerput: The Way We Genuinely Live: Masterworks of Yup'ik Science and Survival*. The catalogue displayed the extraordinary beauty and everyday truth of objects made to be useful by and for Indigenous peoples in Alaska—*made* objects that *make meaning* out of wood and stone and skin and fur and woven fabric. In the Gitxsan community that we have visited several times in this book, snowshoes are necessary for survival as well as success in winter. Traditional snowshoe makers themselves tell a story or sing a song for every step of the way—from the shaping of the wood (usually alder) to each and every different knot tied for webbing (usually made from deer or moose hide). And those stories become one with the snowshoes. In every way of life and in every workplace, there are techniques and tools and working tackle that tell such stories.

And you have to *believe* in them, says Mestokosho. He was talking about his elders, but he would have included all the crafts and all the stories that kept them in a good way. I once heard Yup'ik fishers in Alaska tell how when they were growing up they were taught to listen to stories about fishing off the coast so carefully that if a fly landed on their nose they were not to brush it off because if they lost their concentration and didn't get the words exactly right, in exactly the right order, they would miss the harbour or offend the spirits or both. Order is everything in navigation, as it is in stories and songs. Order is beauty and order conveys truth. Order is style and spirit. These stories were to the fishers like rosary beads, guiding them through. We hear something of this spirit in the exhausting insistence of children that we remember the precise words in the precise order in a story we are telling—perhaps one of their favourites—that we have told them before. If we make a mistake, we will be called to account and forced to make a correction. I think there is, more than we realize, something spiritual in this childhood instinct, something along the lines of those rosary beads. Something about the truth and beauty of life itself.

★ ★ ★

The relative importance of the false and the true in some kinds of storytelling varies over time—sometimes over a very short time. Consider the following three statements made within twenty years of each other. First, there is the poet Matthew Arnold in the 1860s, proposing that the storytelling of art and the criticism that interprets it is "to see the object as in itself it really is." In the 1870s, the literary and art critic Walter Pater changed this to "know one's own impression as it really is." By the 1880s, Oscar Wilde was insisting that the function of art and interpretive storytelling was "to see the object as in itself it really is *not*"—an ambition that twentieth-century science has certainly satisfied.

It is worth picking up the importance of style here, and its relationship with what I just called *order*, keeping Oscar Wilde's insistence that truth-telling is a matter of style in mind. Style in storytelling is an elusive but almost always recognizable quality, as it is in Einstein's wonderful equation and in Keats's poem. We can say that style is just on the surface. But what is on the surface is not necessarily superficial. And style goes much deeper than the surface in storytelling. In the nineteenth century, they talked about style and truth in the same breath, with art critics speaking of the *virtù*—the essential being—of Renaissance painting.

Style in the arts and elsewhere is also shaped by ceremonies that are grounded in time and place and culture. In the case of storytelling, some form of style essentially begins all the ceremonies of language, illuminating the ways in which thinking and feeling are inseparable from the languages in which they are communicated. Our thoughts and feelings, and with them what we recognize as truths and beauties, are fundamentally determined by language—or, in the shorthand I have been using, shaped by words and the ways in which they are put together to make meaning. Which is to say: our thoughts and feelings, along with our ideals of truth and beauty, come not just from our hearts and minds but also from our languages.

Sooner or later, truth and beauty always seem to come back to language, and so does belief. The connection between words and images and thoughts and feelings is both exciting and unsettling. And that excitement and unease go back a long way. During the seventeenth and eighteenth centuries, notable European scientists and scholars such as Gottfried Leibniz, fresh from the co-invention of calculus with Isaac Newton, argued that verbal language in particular was not just a tool for communication but a fundamental determinant of thought, feeling and behaviour. Leibniz was soon joined by an enthusiastic chorus, and in the late eighteenth century, the idea prompted wide discussion and spirited disagreement that has lasted to the present. Language began to be recognized as a trickster as well as a trader in truths. The "prison-house" of language, Wordsworth (and some time later Friedrich Nietzsche) called it. Which was to say words matter, and shape (or mis-shape) our world more than we might realize.

In the early twentieth century, this notion was given a new profile by the anthropologist Franz Boas when he insisted that learning Indigenous languages in the field was fundamental to understanding the cultures and personalities, as well as the sciences, religions and arts of a people. An earlier generation of anthropologists before Boas, such as James Frazer of *The Golden Bough* fame, had mostly stayed on the verandah reading Greek and writing English (or some other European language). But linguists such as Boas's student Edward Sapir, and Sapir's student Benjamin Whorf, helped foster a wider appreciation of how we "know" the world according to the arbitrary categories or "orderings" of different languages, none more arbitrary than our own. This knowledge includes how we define and identify truth, what we believe, and what we consider beautiful.

Linguistic relativity, as it became known, was then given wide currency in the English-speaking world by Samuel Hayakawa in a very popular mid-twentieth-century book called *Language in Thought and Action.* The spirit of scientific relativity that had been popularized by Einstein and others was then turned into a contemporary catchphrase by Marshall McLuhan: The medium is the message. Or as McLuhan also said (in the spirit of Leibniz and Newton): we shape our tools—of which language is certainly one of our most important—and then our tools shape us.

The idea of language *in action* had a history in storytelling, for it was the burden of William Wordsworth's famous collection, in collaboration with Samuel Taylor Coleridge, of what they called *Lyrical Ballads.* Wordsworth wrote a Preface for this book that promoted a storytelling of verbal action rather than visual representation, one that rendered words "part of the passion" rather than just symbols of it. Words as "things, active and efficient," as part of "language in action," was an idea that contributed to the interest by early-twentieth-century linguists in what were called "speech acts," a phrase Hayakawa echoed in the title of his book. It also reinforced the idea that storytelling constituted, rather than simply described, reality, in the same way that constitutions, another form of storytelling language in action, bring a nation into being. Words shaping our world. It was along these lines that the twentieth-century Jewish Romanian-German poet Paul Celan said that for him there was "no difference between a handshake and a poem."

Linguist Benjamin Whorf suggested some other radical perspectives. Comparing the Hopi Pueblo language

169

with a cluster of languages that he called Standard Average European and bringing his training as an engineer to bear on the consequences of speech, he observed, "Experience more basic than language tells us that, if energy is expended, effects are produced." Then he extended this to the possibility that "thought, like any other force, leaves everywhere traces of effect." In saying this, Whorf was challenging the routine assumption, at least for those of us who speak languages of Indo-European lineage, that when we think of something—a specific plant, say, or an animal—we are thinking of it only as an abstract image, a representative sign, rather than as a real object of our actions, mental as well as physical.

We assume that our languages, and the categorical imperatives they impose on us, inevitably diminish our appreciation of the world we live in and of each other, though we try to recover some of our agency with prayers and curses, whose verbal energy we hope will produce the light or darkness of good or bad happenings. But Whorf explains how unnecessarily limited our notions of both reality and our independence of it may be, by showing how for sophisticated people such as the Hopi, it is no more unnatural to think that thought contacts everything and pervades the universe than to think, as we do, that candlelight does this.

According to the logic that we apply to physical action, Whorf argues, it becomes quite reasonable to assume that thought will leave a trace. And yet when *we* think of a rosebush, for example, most of us don't assume that our thoughts go *to* that rosebush and engage with it, like a light turned upon it. What then do we suppose we are doing when we are thinking of a rosebush? Well, Whorf suggested, whatever we call it, we are assigning mental action to a space that is full of representations of the real thing, a space where reality is brought to life in our imagination—which is, after all, where we find truth. But if this is so, surely that thought, that "language act," has some effect and produces some re-action. In his words,

> a Hopi would naturally suppose that his
> thought traffics with the actual rosebush—or
> more likely [for a Hopi] the corn plant—that
> he is thinking about. The thought then should
> leave some trace of itself with the plant in the
> field. If it is a good thought, one about health
> and growth, it is good for the plant; if a bad
> thought, the reverse. And if the corn plant
> is crucial to survival, then thought as well as
> action are implicated.

The startling image of these substantial "traces" of thought and language in action brings to mind John Lubbock, thinking his "first feeling would be one of delight and interest rather than surprise, if some day when I am alone in a wood one of the trees were to speak to me." Traces could, and perhaps do, go both ways. A wise fool, John Lubbock sometimes was. And we know he admired and welcomed that kind of wisdom, especially about scientific things like the natural life of stones and potatoes.

However surprising Whorf's account of the sensitive rosebush may be, people have believed something like it for millennia, using it—as we all use our languages, and the ideas they shape—to survive. And when we are inhibited by a language with discrete subjects and objects and definitive verbs and nouns like the ones I am using, the uncertainty introduced by the Hopi story reminds us that whatever our language, we are all more or less at sea when it comes to the truth about what we call reality. When we turn to truth-telling about the world we live in, our languages offer us something like the tools of navigation that ocean-going sailors used for so long—tools that come with their own uncertainties and contradictions and invitations to believe the unbelievable. And to believe in the ultimate truth of arrival.

★ ★ ★

Belief and Truth. When they come together in storytelling, even if only for a moment, they will surprise us. That surprising moment, whether of delight or dread, can be very precious—a heritage, perhaps, of that first very human moment when language came into being in a word or an image. And any contradictions or uncertainties that accompany that surprise may offer a special kind of pleasure, like the pleasure of learning about "happenings that are not happening" in our early years. The cries of "Eureka" and "Hallelujah" belong to *us*, as well as to science and religion. The surprise moment also ages well, coming back no matter how many times we hear the same story.

Often that moment of surprise celebrates the very contradiction it defies, such as when "once upon a time" becomes "right now." When the Rasta elder told the

Jamaican National Commission on Ganja that "Moses did not see God *in* the burning bush, he saw God *by burning* the bush," he knew he was challenging their ability to believe and not believe at the same time. "Hallelujah!" responded the commissioners, surprising themselves in a moment of genuine delight with a word that not coincidentally celebrated the Rasta name Jah, for God incarnate. Leonard Cohen is reported to have once said, "This world is full of conflicts and full of things that cannot be reconciled. But there are moments when we can reconcile and embrace the whole mess, and that's what I mean by 'Hallelujah.'" That's truth and belief. And beauty.

Joy Harjo introduced us to the tricksters Coyote and Rabbit back in Chapter One in a search for grace that brought a promise of balance. It's time to bring one of them back to join those other tricksters, language and truth, in a poem by my mischievous friend and for five wonderful years my colleague at the University of Toronto, the Acoma Pueblo poet Simon Hihdruutsi Ortiz. The poem is called "The Creation, According to Coyote," a trickster who takes story and song seriously. And like most storytellers Coyote loves boasting and toasting, in this case about the beginnings of life. As a trickster he also loves truth-telling. And like other storytellers, the truths he tells are full of contradictions and uncertainties. Rumours and such, he says, just "hearsay." And the words he uses are strange. But in the beginning, at creation, *of course* the words would be strange, and contradictions and uncertainties would begin there too. Then there was human life—young, and then older—and some exciting and colourful and tragic things of adventure,

and wonders and wonderings and more words. And belief.
Pure and simple belief. Belief in a true story from Grandpa,
who is the storyteller's uncle, and from Coyote, the storytelling maker of meaning in the world. And uncertainty
about whether it is the story or the storyteller, his uncle or
Coyote, that he believes.

"First of all, it's all true."
Coyote, he says this, this way,
humble yourself, motioning and meaning
what he says.

You were born when you came
from that body, the earth;
your black head burst from granite,
the ashes cooling,

until it began to rain.
It turned muddy then,
and then green and brown things
came without legs.

They looked strange.
Everything was strange.
There was nothing to know then,

until later, Coyote told me this,
and he was b.s.-ing probably,
two sons were born,
Uyuyayeh and Masaweh.

They were young then,
and then later on they were older.

And then the people were wondering
what was above.
They had heard rumours.

But, you know, Coyote,
he was mainly bragging
when he said (I think),
"My brothers, the Twins then said,
'Let's lead these poor creatures
and save them.'"

And later on, they came to light
after many exciting and colourful
and tragic things of adventure;
and this is the life, all these, all these.

My uncle told me all this, that time.
Coyote told me too, but you know
how he is, always talking to the gods,
the mountains, the stone all around.

And you know, I believe him.

Endnotes

CHAPTER ONE

Ras Kumi wrote a remarkable theological memoir in the late 1960s titled *The Earth Most Strangest Man: The Rastafarian*. It was later transcribed and printed by Lambros Comitas, director of the Research Institute for the Study of Man in New York and a close friend of Kumi's, but has had limited circulation beyond the Rastafarian community in Jamaica. With Kumi's permission I published excerpts in an issue of the British publication *Index on Censorship* (4/1999) that I co-edited. The Majorcan storyteller's opening is highlighted by Roman Jakobson in his essay "Linguistics and Poetics" from *Language in Literature* (Harvard University Press, 1987). The Khoekhoe words here and later in the book were provided by Levi Namaseb, who makes an appearance in Chapter Five and is the presiding spirit behind much of my work with Khoisan (Bushman) storytellers. Dan Yashinsky's Romanian grandmother appears in several of his essays, and his inspiring insight into storytelling is available in his book *Suddenly They Heard Footsteps: Storytelling for the Twenty-first Century* (Knopf Canada, 2004), which I quote from in Chapter Two. Marshall McLuhan's comment is from *The Gutenberg Galaxy: The Making of Typographic Man* (University of Toronto Press, 1962). The Faroese proverb "bound is the boatless man" is taken from the *Faroe Isles*

Review, whose first few years of publication (beginning in 1976) provide a wealth of information about the islands. The story of the word *cyulis* was told to me by Ian and Dave McDougall of the Dictionary of Old English project at the University of Toronto. Seamus Heaney's phrase about a "buoyancy" and a "holding" comes from *Crediting Poetry: The Nobel Lecture* (Farrar, Straus and Giroux, 1996). C.S. Lewis's comment about the wound and the privilege of individuality is from *An Experiment in Criticism* (Cambridge University Press, 1961). Lewis also makes the point that stories need listeners and readers as much as we need stories—so there's another kind of balance. Oscar Wilde's comment, like several others in the same spirit that I quote in this book, is from his essay "The Decay of Lying," first published in the journal *Nineteenth Century* in January, 1889, and included in his collection of essays titled *Intentions* (Heinemann and Balestier, 1891). My discussion of "wonder" has benefitted from conversations and correspondence over the years with Sean Kane at Trent University. My brief catalogue of the beginnings of our human species owes much to Sander Gilman's splendid discussion of human development in *Stand Up Straight: A History of Posture* (Reaktion Books, 2018) and to his analysis of humanity's later storytelling about, and stereotyping of, Them and Us in his many articles and books, beginning with *Seeing the Insane* (Wiley, 1982), *Difference and Pathology: Stereotypes of Sexuality, Race and Madness* (Cornell University Press, 1985), *Disease and Representation* (Cornell University Press, 1988) and, most recently, with Zhou Xun, *I Know Who Caused Covid-19: Pandemics and Xenophobia* (Reaktion Books, 2021). The final words of that book tell the story: "I know who caused COVID-19. *They* did." Thoreau's comment is from *Walden; or, Life in the Woods* (Ticknor and Fields, 1854). The full title of Paul Veyne's book is

Did the Greeks Believe in Their Myths? An Essay on the Constitutive Imagination, trans. by Paula Wissing (University of Chicago Press, 1988). Joy Harjo's prose poem "Grace" is from her book *In Mad Love and War* (Wesleyan University Press, 1990).

CHAPTER TWO

Jonathan Foer's remark is from "Why a Haggadah?," *New York Times Book Review*, April 1, 2012. The Rastafarian interpretation of the Bible as what Samuel Taylor Coleridge once called "a science of realities" mirrors the Passover injunction that in each generation Jews *realize* that they themselves came out of Egypt and enact this in the Seder. Wordsworth's line is from his poem "The Prelude: Book 1." John Steffler's lines are from his poem "Towers and Monuments" in *The Wreckage of Play* (McClelland and Stewart, 1988), which also opened the anthology *Wild on the Crest: Poems of the Sea*, eds. Mary Dalton, Kristina Fagan, Ken Munro and Peter Walsh (Jeroboam Books, 1995). I gave details about Dan Yashinsky's book in the endnote for Chapter One. The story of the grizzly Madiik and the mudslide on the mountain called Stekyawden was told to me many times by the late Neil Sterritt, who led the Gitxsan and Wet'suwet'en in their landmark legal case called *Delgamuukw*, discussed in Chapter Five. Neil, a traditional Gitxsan who trained as a geologist, also told me about his decision to turn to geology and about using core sample dating to balance the two stories in the trial. The anecdote about Jacobsen is from J.B. Leishman and Stephen Spender's introduction to the *Duino Elegies* of Rainer Maria Rilke (Hogarth Press, 1952). The idea of those "momentary gods" was developed within the mythical and spiritual framework of early humanity proposed by linguists, most prominently Max Müller in books such as *Lectures on the Science of Religion* (Charles Scribner and Company, 1872) and Otto Jesperson in *Progress in Language* (Macmillan and Company, 1894) and was taken up in the twentieth century by philosophers Ernst Cassirer in *An Essay on Man: An Introduction to a Philosophy of Human Culture* (Yale University Press, 1944) and Suzanne K. Langer, who translated *Language and Myth* (Harper and Brothers, 1946). In many of these books, albeit in different ways, there are traces of Indigenous and settler spiritual beliefs that in the beginning there was a word or an image. E.H. Gombrich's book *A Little History of the World* was first published in German in 1936 and then 1985, and translated into English by Caroline Mustill (Yale University Press, 2008). Ralph Waldo Emerson's remark about the fossilization of words is from his essay "The Poet," collected in *Essays: Second Series* (James Munroe and Company, 1844). William Carlos Williams's lines are from a fragment he titled "My Luv," discussed by Hasine Sen Karadeniz of Istanbul University in her article "No Ideas But in Things: William Carlos Williams' Objectivist Poetry," *LITERA, Journal of Western Languages and Literatures* (2009). Michael Ondaatje's "The Cinnamon Peeler's Wife" is from *Running in the Family* (McClelland and Stewart, 1982) and Lorna Goodison's "Guinea Woman" from *I Am Becoming My Mother* (New Beacon Books, 1986). John Polanyi's observation is from his essay "The Magic of Science," published in both the *Imperial Oil Review* (Spring, 1994) and the *Canadian Federation for the Humanities Bulletin* (1994). William Ernest Henley was lying in an Edinburgh hospital fighting to save his one remaining leg from amputation—he had lost the other when he was sixteen—when he wrote his poem "Invictus," and it was there and in that condition that he somehow found the courage to portray his experiences in this harrowingly realistic lyric that celebrates the survival of the human spirit. T.S. Eliot's collection of essays *The Sacred Wood: Essays on Poetry and Criticism* was published by Methuen in 1920. Francis James Child's *The English and Scottish Popular Ballads* were published in five volumes by Houghton Mifflin and Company between 1882 and 1898. John Lomax's book *Cowboy Songs and Other Frontier Ballads* was published in 1910. Donald Akenson's comment is from *God's Peoples: Covenant and Land in South Africa, Israel and Ulster* (Cornell University Press, 1992), a book which ends with the prediction that what he calls a covenantal cosmology, founded on spiritual belief, "will be one of the most effective ways for a myriad of small nations to fortify themselves in a world that will increasingly be confusion and whirl." The story about the stern rebuke to Walter Scott from James Hogg's mother was told by Stuart McHardy in his essay "The Story of Story and a Canon of Story" in *Or Words to That Effect: Orality and the Writing of Literary History*, eds. Daniel F. Chamberlain and J. Edward Chamberlin (John Benjamins, 2016). Richard and Nora Marks Dauenhauer, eminent scholars of Tlingit oral performance, wrote (echoing Ralph Waldo Emerson) that "the writing down of oral performance, no matter how well intentioned or how well carried out, petrifies it. It is like a molecule by molecule replacement of an organic plant by stone. A petrified log may look like wood, but it is actually stone," from "Oral Literature Embodied and Disembodied," in *Aspects of Oral Communication*, ed. M. Quasthoff (De Gruyter, 1995). Then they defied their own prediction in a multi-volume series of *Classics of Tlingit Oral Literature* (University of Washington Press, 1987–2008) that brought orality back to life. Virginia Woolf's comment on "a change in human nature" is from her essay *Mr. Bennett and Mrs. Brown*, published by Hogarth Press in 1924. There is a discussion of the Grafton Gallery exhibition and its impact in Samuel Hynes's book *The Edwardian Turn of Mind* (Princeton University Press, 1968). Confucius's instruction is from his *Analects*, Chapter 13. Jacob Thomas told me his story about reciting the Great Law of the Haudenosaunee in translation. Vine Deloria Jr. gave the Lakota Sioux elder his storytelling name, Fred. And gave me stern advice about the protocols of permission for Indigenous stories. His book *Custer Died for Your Sins: An Indian Manifesto* (MacMillan, 1969) opened up fundamental questions about American western expansion and Native American history.

CHAPTER THREE

My visit to CERN was in the fall of 2017. Isaiah spoke these words in Chapter 40, verse 4, of *The Book of the Prophet Isaiah* (in the King James Version of the Bible). Charles Darwin's "truly poetical" conclusion is from his notebook entry written in 1838, having landed back in England from his great journey of discovery to the Galapagos (among other places) in 1836; and it is quoted by Sandra Herbert in *Charles Darwin, Geologist* (Cornell University Press, 2005). Lewis Hyde's *Trickster Makes This World: Mischief, Myth and Art* was published in 1998 by Farrar, Straus and Giroux. My identification of the author and date of "Home on the Range" comes from one of the most knowledgeable scholars (and performers) of cowboy songs, Hal Cannon, who wrote in his collection of *Old Time Cowboy Songs* (Gibbs Smith, 1988) that "about a hundred people have claimed authorship, but it looks like it was first penned in 1873 by Brewster Higby from Índiana." Hal Cannon is also one of the founders of the very popular annual "National Cowboy Poetry Gathering" in Elko, Nevada. David Olson illuminates the distinction between Polynesian and European navigation in *The World on Paper* (Cambridge University Press, 1994). The term "wayfinders" has had a long history, though its use by Wade Davis as the title of his book *Wayfinders: Why Ancient Wisdom Matters in the Modern World* (House of Anansi Press, 2009) gave it new currency; and Davis's discussion of Polynesian seafaring is as well founded as his many other chronicles of exploration. Patrick Nunn has opened up new lines of inquiry in books such as *Oceanic Islands* (Wiley, 1994) and *Vanished Islands and Hidden Continents of the Pacific* (University of Hawai'i Press, 2008), offering a chronology of settlement on Polynesian islands that includes the grim consequences of climate change throughout the centuries. And Greg Dening's writing about the navigation of the Polynesian seas in *Islands and Beaches* (Dorsey Press, 1980) and *Readings/ Writings* (Melbourne University Press, 1998) and in articles such as "Geographical Knowledge of the Polynesians and the Nature of Inter-Island Contact" in *Polynesian Navigation* (1962, ed. Jack Golson) have influenced almost everyone who has taken up the subject. My comments about the seafaring origins of the words "disorientation" and "desnorteados" come from Donald S. Johnson's *Phantom Islands of the Atlantic* (Walker and Company, 1994), where I also learned about medieval seafaring adventurers losing civil rights on their return. Robert Finley's book *The Accidental Indies* was published in 2000 by McGill-Queen's University Press, and in French translation won the Governor General's Award in 2004. Finley published a version of his elegiac description of dead reckoning as "Reading the View: On the Opening of the Crowfoot Library" in *Alberta Views* (Summer, 2004), and he wrote about riddling in his essay "The Riddles Charm," *Dalhousie Review* (Autumn, 1997). I also benefitted greatly from Finley's discussions of the many other uncertainties of language in his 1989 University of Toronto doctoral thesis on *Difficult Language in the Poetry and W.S. Merwin*. Andrew Welsh's *The Roots of Lyric* was published in 1978 by Princeton University Press. My commentary on the wonders of mathematics was first influenced by my teachers, especially Tony Parker-Jervis at St. George's School and Nathan Divinsky at UBC. And by Lucienne Felix in *The Modern Aspect of Mathematics*, translated by Julius H. Hlavaty and Fancille H. Hlavaty (Basic Books Inc., 1960); Morris Kline's *Mathematics in Western Culture* (Oxford University Press, 1953); Ivan Niven's *Numbers: Rational and Irrational* (Random House, 1961); and William Dunham's *Journey Through Genius: The Great Theorems of Mathematics* (Wiley, 1990). The definition of infinity as "a place where things happen that don't" is also attributed to an unidentified schoolboy by Eli Maor in *To Infinity and Beyond: A Cultural History of the Infinite* (Princeton University Press, 1991). Scott Buchanan's book *Poetry and Mathematics* (University of Chicago Press, 1962) brings storytelling and mathematics together in very persuasive ways. One writer not usually credited with an interest in mathematics is the literary critic Northrop Frye, who wrote about it surprisingly often, celebrating mathematics as a richly imaginative form of storytelling, and concluding his landmark *Anatomy of Criticism* (Princeton University Press, 1957) by paying tribute to the foundational association of literature with mathematics, proposing that "literature, like mathematics, is a language, and language in itself represents no truth though it may provide the means for expressing any number of them," adding that "we have always believed in some kind of imaginative truth, and perhaps the justification for the belief is in the containment by the language of what it can express. The mathematical and verbal universes are doubtless different ways of conceiving the same universe." And in case we might think that mathematics is an exclusive inheritance from European and Asian culture, the book *Native American Mathematics*, edited by Michael P. Closs (University of Texas Press, 1986) brings together mathematical theory and practice from a wide range of Indigenous mathematical traditions and from an equally wide range of times and places. Matthew Arnold's *Culture and Anarchy: An Essay in Political and Social Criticism* (Smith, Elder and Company, 1869) began as a lecture that he delivered as Professor of Poetry at Oxford in 1867 and called "Culture and Its Enemies." My commentary on Edmund Burke is much indebted to Stephen Regan's introduction to his *Irish Writing: An Anthology of Irish Literature in English 1789–1939* (Oxford University Press, 2004). Wilde's celebration of disobedience was written in his essay "The Soul of Many Under Socialism," published in the *Fortnightly Review* (February, 1891). Annie Ned's comment about "a talk from Grandpa" is from Julie Cruikshank's *Do Glaciers Listen? Local Knowledge, Colonial Encounters, and Social Imagination* (UBC Press, 2005).

CHAPTER FOUR

Robert Schumann's comment is from George Steiner's *Real Presences* (University of Chicago Press, 1989). Along with Michael Chapman, Edgard Sienaert has translated Piet Draghoender's lament in ways that reflect Marcel Jousse's theories of storytelling—shaped by the place where we live, our physical and natural environment, and our innately human performative gestures. An account of Piet's performance was published by Jeffrey B. Peires in a University of the Witwatersrand History Workshop booklet in 1987. Bob Marley's seven-word statement by the Jamaican leader Marcus Garvey, speaking at Liberty Hall in Nova Scotia in 1937, is repeated in Marley's "Redemption Song." George Woodcock and Ivan Avakumovic's book *The Doukhobors* (Faber and Faber, 1968) offers a sympathetic and historically responsible account of the Doukhobor story. My remarks on the musical form of the Doukhobor singing that I heard in Victory Square is from Kenneth Peacock's introduction to *Songs of the Doukhobors* (Queen's Printer for Canada, 1970). The words of Bronislaw Malinowski that I quoted are from his essay "The Meaning of Meaningless Words and the Coefficient of Weirdness," published in his book *Coral Gardens and Their Magic*, Vol. 2: *The Language of Magic and Gardening* (George Allen and Unwin, 1935). Kris Kristofferson's words are from "Me and Bobby McGee"; Elton John's from "Sad Songs Say So Much"; Jimmie Rodgers's from "T.B. Blues"; and Hank Williams's from "I'm So Lonesome I Could Cry." Hart Crane's line is from his poem "Chaplinesque," published in *White Buildings* (Boni and Liveright, 1926). Michael Asch's success in negotiating the agreement that brought Smithsonian Folkways into being and gave new life to the principles and dedication that inspired his father's remarkable achievement are presented in a marvellous 26-episode radio and podcast series narrated by Michael that celebrates the nearly 2,200 LP recordings made by Folkways (each with extensive liner notes) and the musical traditions from around the world that they represent. Derek Walcott's lines are from his poem "The Schooner Flight," in *The Star-Apple Kingdom* (Farrar, Straus and Giroux, 1980). Thomas Hardy's poem "The Oxen" was first published in the London *Times* on Christmas Eve, 1915. Wordsworth's account of that "state of almost savage torpor" is from his preface to the *Lyrical Ballads* (T.N. Longman and G. Rees, 1800). John Keats's poem "Ode to a Nightingale" was written in the spring of 1819 and published in *Annals of the Fine Arts* the following July. George Herbert's memorable lines are from his poem "Prayer I," published in *The Temple* (Cambridge, 1633). The founder and director of the Ceremonial Grounds at CAMH is the Mohawk elder and traditional healer Kahontakwas Diane Longboat. Eduardo Galeano's advice is from his essay "The Imagination and the Will to Change," translated by Mariana Valverde in *The Writer and Human Rights* (Lester and Orpen Dennys, 1983) from the transcript of a speech he gave at a 1983 conference in Vancouver. Eduardo Duran has since written a book about his work, titled *Healing the Soul Wound: Trauma-Informed Counseling for Indigenous Communities* (Teachers College Press, 2019). The gathering in Saskatchewan was organized as part of an International Summer Institute in 1996, directed by the distinguished Mi'kmaq educator Marie Battiste at the University of Saskatchewan, and chronicled in a book she edited, titled *Reclaiming Indigenous Voice and Vision* (UBC Press, 2000).

CHAPTER FIVE

McLuhan's offhand remark is from *The Gutenberg Galaxy* (University of Toronto Press, 1962). Walter Ong's *Orality and Literacy: The Technologizing of the Word* was first published by Routledge in 1982, and there is a long list of those who sing in chorus with Ong, from classicists to cognitive psychologists. One among the latter who sings on his own, and with rare insight, is David Olson, especially in his book *The World on Paper* (Cambridge University Press, 1994) and in a number of articles since. There is a wonderful account of the Chauvet paintings in *Dawn of Art: The Chauvet Caves* by Jean-Marie Chauvet, Eliette Brunel Deschamps and Christian Hillaire (Harry N. Abrams, 1996). And a very powerful video documentary by Werner Herzog titled *Cave of Forgotten Dreams* (2010). Thomas King's book *The Inconvenient Indian* was published in 2012 by Doubleday Canada. Bartolomé de las Casas wrote his own *History of the Indies*, which was first published in English in 1971 by Harper and Row. The most expansive accounts of las Casas and his legacy are Lewis Hanke's *Aristotle and the American Indian* (Henry Regnery Company, 1959) and *All Mankind Is One: A Study of the Disputation between Bartolomé de Las Casas and Juan Gines de Sepulveda in 1550 on the Intellectual and Religious Capacity of the American Indians* (Northern Illinois University Press, 1974). Helen Hunt Jackson's *A Century of Dishonor*, first published in 1881, chronicled the brutal mistreatment, broken treaties and forced removal of Indigenous peoples in the United States going back to 1776. It was widely read at the time, and for a brief while prompted lively debate in the House of Commons about Canada's dishonourable conduct...but little changed in either country. My own book, *The Harrowing of Eden: White Attitudes Towards Native Americans* (1975) picked up the story. Thomas Berger gives a compelling account of las Casas and the legacy of 1492 at the beginning of his book *A Long and Terrible Shadow: White Values, Native Rights in the Americas* (Douglas & McIntyre, 1991). John Rastell's poem was published in *Tudor Facsimile Texts*, ed. John S. Farmer, Vol. 85 (London, 1908). I am grateful to my colleague and Renaissance scholar Anne Lancashire for Rastell's literary background. Details of the *Delgamuukw* case are available in a book of excerpts, cartoons and commentary from the trial, compiled by Don Monet and Skanu'u (Ardythe Wilson) and titled *Colonialism on Trial: Indigenous Land Rights and the Gitksan and Wet'suwet'en Sovereignty Case* (New Society Publishers, 1992), and in the Supreme Court judgment of December 11, 1997. Neil Sterritt's *Mapping My Way Home: A Gitxsan History* was published by Creekstone Press in 2016. At Neil's request, I wrote the foreword. The last line of the *Iliad* that I quote is from the 1882 prose translation by Andrew Lang, Walter Leaf and Ernest Myers, which was standard fare when I was in school. Don McKay's poem "Fates Worse Than Death" was published in *Apparatus* (McClelland and Stewart, 1997) and later collected in *Camber: Selected Poems* (McClelland and Stewart, 2004). In addition to the respect he received from the Rastafarian community, Barry Chevannes's reputation as an exceptionally perceptive scholar of Rastafari was confirmed with his book *Rasta: Roots and Ideology* (Syracuse University Press, 1995). When I think of the elder from Montego Bay, who transformed the Ganja Commission with his story of Moses burning the bush, I am reminded of a comment by Ras Kumi at the beginning of his spiritual memoir *The Earth Most Strangest Man: The Rastafarian*. "I an I worship from the

Bible but do not worship the Bible." Which is to say, we tell our own stories. The story of John Lubbock, and his stories of the Manchester woman and the Norwich countryman, are from a two-volume *Life of Sir John Lubbock* (Macmillan and Co., 1914) by Horace G. Hutchinson. Lubbock died in 1913.

CHAPTER SIX

Barre Toelken's story is from his article "Sleeping with Both Eyes" in *Native Arts Issues 81/82*, ed. Suzi Jones, published by the Alaska State Council on the Arts (1982). He and Larry Evers edited a book titled *Native American Oral Traditions: Collaboration and Interpretation* (Utah State University Press, 2001) that brings together some inspiring stories. John Keats' lines about beauty and truth are from his "Ode on a Grecian Urn." Wallace Stevens's poem "The Idea of Order at Key West" is from his book *Ideas of Order* (Alfred A. Knopf, 1936). Jacob Bronowski's celebration of the imagination in the sciences and the arts is from his essay "The Imaginative Mind in Science" in *The Visionary Eye: Essays in the Arts, Literature and Science*, selected and edited by Piero E. Ariotti in collaboration with Rita Bronowski (MIT Press, 1978). For more on Pythagoras and his round earth, see an article in the *American Physical Society (APS) News*, Vol. 15, No. 6, June 2006. The distinction proposed by J.B.S. Haldane is from his essay on "Science and Theology as Art Forms" in *The New Criticism: An Anthology of Modern Aesthetics and Literary Criticism*, ed. Edwin P. Burgum (Prentice-Hall, 1930). Tuzo Wilson's career and contributions are often recounted by his colleagues at the University of Toronto and are reported in the *Canadian Encyclopedia* (1958, online since 1999). The English translation of Serge Bouchard's *Caribou Hunter: A Song of a Vanished Innu Life* (Greystone Books, 2006) was by Joan Irving. Ann Fienup-Riordan's *Yuungnaqpiallerput: The Way We Genuinely Live: Masterworks of Yup'ik Science and Survival* was published in 2007 by the University of Washington Press. Matthew Arnold's comment was made at the beginning of his essay "The Function of Criticism at the Present Time"; Pater's in his *Studies in the History of the Renaissance* (Macmillan and Co., 1873); and Wilde's in his essay "The Critic as Artist." Samuel Hayakawa's book *Language in Thought and Action* was published in 1949 by Harcourt, Brace and World. These views of Wordsworth about language are also presented in the third of his *Essays upon Epitaphs* (1810). Richard Sanger drew particular attention to Wordsworth's poetic "language in action" in his 1994 University of Toronto doctoral thesis on *Direct Speech and Narrative in Four Twentieth Century Poets: Lorca, Auden, Borges and Walcott*. Scott Marentette quoted the remark by Paul Celan in his 2010 University of Toronto doctoral thesis *The Language of Real Life: Self-Possession in the Poetry of Paul Celan, T.S. Eliot, Rainer Maria Rilke, and Paul Valery*. Benjamin Lee Whorf's discussion is in *Language, Thought and Reality*, a selection of his writings edited by John B. Carroll in 1956. The Leonard Cohen quotation is taken from an interview with him by John McKenna, RTE Ireland, May 9 and 12, 1988, transcribed by Martin Godwyn. Simon Hihdruutsi Ortiz's poem first appeared in the magazine *Dacotah Territory* in the early 1970s and was then published as the first poem in *Going for the Rain* (Harper and Row, 1976). It also begins his collection *Woven Stone* (University of Arizona Press, 1992 & 2022).

Acknowledgements

STORYLINES would not have come to life were it not for my wife, Lorna Goodison, who put up with my false starts, my foolish delusions about being finished, and my general grumbling and groaning. I thank her for her faith and fortitude, her encouragement and support, her helpful and healing advice, and her love.

The book began with a seminar course I taught for three years after my retirement at the University of Toronto, thanks to an invitation from Victoria College Principals David Cook and Angela Esterhammer. I called the course How Stories Work. It turned out that even after forty years of teaching literature I didn't really know. But I did have some thoughts, and in the genial and generous company of a couple of dozen students each year, from a wide range of disciplines and many of the professional faculties, we worked our way towards some tentative ideas, enriched by their linguistic and cultural traditions and by their own storytelling. I am deeply grateful to them for their patience, their persistence, and their confidence—not only in me, but also in their own experiences and insights.

But of course it all began much earlier, with the stories my mother would tell and the songs my father would sing, each full of the mischief and the mystery of their own personalities. At the time I almost certainly thought more about the storytelling than I did about them, so it's time to make up for that. This book is written in their memory.

My manuscript became a book thanks to Howard White and Anna Comfort O'Keeffe at Douglas & McIntyre, and it would not have happened were it not for my editor, the incomparable Jennifer Glossop in Toronto. Caroline Skelton, Noel Hudson, Luke Inglis, Dwayne Dobson and their colleagues at Douglas & McIntyre made it ready for publication, and Lohit Jagwani and his crew at Zg Stories helped give it currency in the market.

Along the way, I benefitted from the advice of many friends. Janet Turnbull Irving kept me going through some difficult times, and reassured me when things were going well. Louise Dennys, my publisher and editor until her retirement from Knopf Canada, encouraged me in the early stages of the book and has been a friend for over thirty years. And Dick Harrison, an old friend and for many years director of the Sunshine Coast Arts Council, gave me an encouraging sense of the book's possibility, which was nourished by Bev Shaw at Talewind Books in Sechelt, and Michael and Dale Jackson at the EarthFair bookstore in Madeira Park, who have supported my writing over the years in a variety of ways. Graeme Wynn, John Borrows, Keavy Martin and Lorna read the manuscript in its early stages, giving me indispensable advice. As did Sander Gilman, who was with me every step of the way, as he and his wife Marina have been since we first met at Cornell over fifty years ago, telling stories to our students and to each other. Along with Brian and Linda Corman they are my oldest friends in the academic trade, and their support has been a blessing. John and Barb Murray have also been close company and loyal friends over every one of those years, and I continue to rely on them. You cannot do this alone, even though it is often lonely work. David Naylor supported my work and sung my praises at many crucial moments, and I am grateful for his faith in me and my work. I dearly miss my friends Bill Charlton and John Burns, with their irrepressible spirit of adventure; and George Laforme, who was with me from our schooldays, read everything I wrote, and listened to me. He and his storytelling father inspired me in all kinds of ways, and his family—Dianne, Cliff and Kent—remain dear friends. Ted and Bettie Zinkan brought me into the company of campfire songs, canoe trip stories, cowboy tales, the wonderful Max Ferguson Show on CBC Radio, and the mountains and rivers of the Kootenay and Columbia valleys; and they provided an introduction to several of the Ktunaxa and Secwepemc hunters and gatherers I got to know, men and women supremely confident in their homeland territory even as they struggled to survive on their reserves. Ted and Bettie's son Gaither now keeps me company on the West Coast, having built the house where Lorna and I live. And my sister Liz and brother-in-law Bob Food, along with Britt Ellis, Paddy Stewart, Tim and Nalini Stewart, and Patrick Saul have been supporters and friends for a very long time.

My Jamaican family—especially Karl, Keith and Miles Goodison—have always been there with refreshing enthusiasm, as have Eddie Baugh, Barry Chevannes, Jeffrey Cobham, Elaine Melbourne, Rex Nettleford, Philip Sherlock, Jean Smith, and Jo and Burchell Whiteman. And Ras Kumi's friendship was a blessing.

Outside my family and close friends, many of my teachers at school and university focused my interests. Tony Parker-Jervis at St. George's school and Nathan Divinsky at UBC taught me how to follow the storylines of mathematics, and how to manage the feeling of being lost in its storytelling. And my interest in stories and songs, already well on the way, was fostered by John Hulcoop and Jan deBruyn at UBC; Graham Midgely, Bruce Mitchell, and

Rachel Trickett at Oxford; and Northrop Frye, Kathleen Coburn, Felp Priestley, Milton Wilson, Jerry Bentley and Bill Blissett, at Toronto. Fred Morgan at the *Hudson Review* in New York showed me how wide the world of literature was and always encouraged my work. And in those early days, my sense of Indigenous heritage and history was heightened by working with Kahontakwas Diane Longboat at the University of Toronto, who directed the Aboriginal Health Professions Program and inspired the establishment of First Nations House with its resident elders, spiritual resources and community spirit. Justus George Lawler in New York and Ramsay Derry in Toronto published my first books back in the 1970s, and Ramsay continued to give me excellent editorial advice and encouragement in the years following. Jan-Erik Guerth of Blue Bridge Books in New York edited and published two of my recent books and taught me much about storytelling.

I am grateful to the many other colleagues and friends who have invited or encouraged me to speak and write about storytelling over the years, and supported me when I did: Michael and Margaret Asch, Anthony and Andrea Barale, Diana Bryden, Dan Chamberlain, Lambros Comitas, Lorna Crozier, Julie Cruikshank, Misao Dean, Robert Finley, Chad Gaffield, Reg Greer, Amir Hussain, Derek and Sue Hopkins, Linda Hutcheon, John Jennings, Joerg Jaschinski, Aaron Joe, Harold and Liz Jones, Waboos Bob Kahgee, Sean Kane, Asif Khan, Fanny Kiefer, Anne Lancashire, Patrick Lane, Richard Landon, John Lutz, Ian MacRae, Kate McAll, Don McKay, Mark McLean, Karen Mulhallen, Tak Nakajima, Richard Nelson, Peter Nesselroth, Michael Nightingale, John O'Brian, David Olson, Ian Pitfield, Ato Quayson, Jahan Ramazani, Maggie Redekop Stephen Regam, Bobby Rotenberg, Ann Saddlemyer, Carolyn Servid, Richard Sanger, David Smith,

Paul Stevens, John Straley, John Stubbs, Jacob Thomas, Neil ten Kortenaar, Helen Tiffim, Jim Tully, Heidi Kiiwetinepinesiik Stark, Richard Van Camp, Tom Wayman, Wendy Wickwire and Dan Yashinsky. And at every turn, Val Napoleon and her colleagues at the University of Victoria, who have given me a renewed sense that what I am doing is worthwhile.

In Australia, Adam Shoemaker has been a constant ally, and Naomi Myers and Gary Foley opened many community doors for me when I was there in the 1980s. In South Africa, Duncan Brown, Keyan Tomselli, Peter Vale, Michael Chapman, Edgard Sienaert, the San (Bushmen) of the ǂKhomani community in the Northern Cape, and the scholar and storyteller Levi Namaseb have given much help and generous support. Basil Robinson opened the door for my first—and the government's first serious, albeit hesitant—involvement with land claims when the Council for Yukon Indians submitted its claim in 1973; and he and Geoff Murray, fresh from External Affairs and the United Nations, gave me a sense of how truly inter-national consultation could—and should—work. Thomas Berger asked me to join him in the Mackenzie Valley Pipeline Inquiry, which not only changed my life but much more importantly began the long process of changing Canada by attending to the unfinished business at the heart of our country, of which we were constantly reminded by Lloyd Barber. It was also during those years that I met Neil Sterritt, who became a very close friend and fellow traveller. Both Tom and Neil, in different ways, taught me—or at least tried to teach me—how to listen. A few years later I worked on behalf of the Blueberry River First Nations with lawyers Rick Salter and Art Pape in a breach of trust case that went to, and was successful in, the Supreme Court of Canada. Following this,

I spent a couple of years in close consultation with Dave Porter and Victor Mitander of the Council for Yukon Indians on the threats to their territory from another pipeline project. During the Alaska Native Review Commission, led by Thomas Berger, I participated in a special project designed by Gary Holhaus and Dorik Mechau—a series of roundtable discussions in which settler and Indigenous leaders and scholars exchanged views on political, legal and philosophical issues… and listened to each other. It was a small but important step forward that continues to inspire me, and led to friendships that enriched my life and improved my understanding of both Indigenous and settler stories and songs. When the Dene leader Georges Erasmus, whom I knew from my time in the Mackenzie Valley, became national chief of the Assembly of First Nations, he and I organized a collaborative conference with the AFN and the University of Toronto on Aboriginal self-determination. It brought together Indigenous people from across the Americas and attracted very large attention. A couple of years later, when Georges became co-chair of the Royal Commission on Aboriginal Peoples, he and the director of research, Mohawk leader Marlene Brant Castellano, asked me to join the Royal Commission as senior advisor. Their belief in what I was doing gave me confidence to keep doing it. It was also during this Royal Commission that I had the good fortune to become friends with Paul Chartrand, who was one of the commissioners and has kept me conscious of Métis heritage and homeland.

Such lists are seldom complete, but I hope those who are not mentioned will accept my apologies, and my thanks. And in my Endnotes I try to acknowledge the help that I got from the many storytellers I have only met in books and essays.

All Indigenous stories in this book are told with permission from the Indigenous storytellers. Written permission for use of their poems has been provided by Don McKay and Simon Ortiz, and written permission to use quotations from their writing came from Robert Finley and Stephen Regan, and from Wesleyan University Press on behalf of Joy Harjo. Justin Dowling of Blue Mountain Music and Primary Wave Music provided permission for use of the verse from Bob Marley's song "Chant Down Babylon." Permission to use the quotation from Jacob Bronowski was given by Clare Bronowski on behalf of the Rita Bronowski Trust. Permission to use Eduardo Galeano's words came from the Eduardo Galeano Estate, with the indispensable assistance of Susan Bergholz Literary Services. I am very grateful to them all.

I want to pay special tribute to my godmother, Margaret Williams, who would read to me from the journal her mother kept of her visits to Louis Riel in prison. Even though she knew the journal by heart, she would read it like holy scripture. I also want to salute my cousin Jack Cowdry, who began his working life driving logging trucks down the North Shore mountains and then turned his talents into a very successful transport business based on Granville Island and busy along every road in the province. He was a dedicated reader and a superb storyteller, over the years I learned much from him, and his generous legacy made it possible to build the house in which this book was written, in Shíshálh territory looking out to the Salish Sea.

Finally I want to give heartfelt thanks to the late Jane Clement Chamberlin, who was my companion and friend and supporter for nearly thirty years. With her in mind, this book is dedicated to our children—Sarah, Geoff and Meg—who have encouraged and inspired and directed me for years, and whose friendship I cherish.

About the Author

J. EDWARD CHAMBERLIN is professor emeritus at the University of Toronto and was senior research associate with the Royal Commission on Aboriginal Peoples. He has worked on sovereignty and land claims throughout Canada and around the world, and has spoken widely on literary, historical and cultural issues. He is the author of several acclaimed titles, including *Horse: How the Horse Has Shaped Civilizations* (2006), which was a national bestseller, and *If This Is Your Land, Where Are Your Stories? Finding Common Ground* (2003), both published by Knopf Canada. He is an Officer of the Order of Canada, and now lives in Halfmoon Bay, BC.